"Jammed with helpful stor _____

Ahead serves as a reminder that God's mercy extends not only to adolescents but to those who've been tasked with raising them. Highly recommended."

    David Zahl, Author of *Low Anthropology*; director of Mockingbird Ministries

"*Parenting Ahead* does much more than provide parenting techniques—it will help you understand the heart motivations behind what you and your children do. Hatton provides a scriptural doorway through which to encourage, strengthen, and challenge parents."

    Marty Machowski, Family Pastor; author of *The Ology*, *God Made Boys and Girls*, and *Parenting First Aid*

"Kristen speaks gospel good news to ears ringing from toddler tantrums, inviting them to trade the tactics they use to make it to bedtime for grace and intentionality, cultivating connection instead of choosing convenience, and laying the foundation we need to parent our toddlers as well as our teens."

    Abbey Wedgeworth, Mom of three (loud) little boys; author of *Held* and the Training Young Hearts children's book series

"In *Parenting Ahead*, Kristen Hatton gives moms and dads a rich theological foundation for redemptive parenting and offers practical biblical wisdom, all in a tone of warmth and compassion for parents who want to raise children who love Jesus."

    Anna Meade Harris, Senior Director of Content at Rooted Ministry

"In this winsome and gospel-centered invitation to be forward-thinking about the teen years, Kristen Hatton shows us Jesus and his compassionate pursuit—just the very remedy for our sin-ridden hearts that my husband and I hope to offer our own two girls."

    Holly Mackle, Humor columnist for Lifeway's *HomeLife* magazine; author of *Bright Star: The Story of Esther*

"Backed by Scripture and counseling experience, *Parenting Ahead* offers parents practical ideas and principles that have the power to transform families from the inside out."

    Krista Gilbert, Life coach; author of *Reclaiming Home*; cohost of *The Open Door Sisterhood* podcast

"I found myself nodding in agreement as I read Kristen Hatton's wise words. Her redemptive parenting approach is filled with wisdom, encouragement, humility, compassion, grace, and truth—all qualities children crave from their parents. This practical parenting book is grounded in God's Word. *Parenting Ahead* is the guide parents of teens and preteens need. I highly recommend it."

Lori Wildenberg, Licensed parent and family educator; parent coach; author of *The Messy Life of Parenting*

"As we navigate a complicated time in our world, parents need wise guides and trusted voices offering help and hope for the journey. Kristen brings the experience of a seasoned parent and the wisdom of a trusted counselor to this book. It is a needed resource."

David Thomas, Therapist; best-selling author of *Raising Emotionally Strong Boys* and *Are My Kids on Track?*

"While Kristen reminds us there is no perfect parenting formula, in *Parenting Ahead* she offers helpful perspective on what does and doesn't matter on this journey. I appreciated her encouragement to keep a long-range mindset and to continue my efforts to intentionally connect and communicate God's gospel love in our day-to-day family moments."

Heather MacFadyen, Host of the *Don't Mom Alone* podcast; author of *Right Where You Belong*

"Kristen Hatton offers up a hope-filled and biblically faithful corrective that helps parents understand the high calling and high privilege of nurturing our kids in the Christian faith. Thank you Kristen for helping us see what it means to parent with grace under God's Word in today's changing and confusing world!"

Walt Mueller, The Center for Parent/Youth Understanding

"In *Parenting Ahead*, Kristen Hatton helps parents be proactive with their younger children so they are better prepared for the changes and challenges of the years to come. Whether your child is two or twelve, every parent will gain important insight."

Meg Meeker, MD, Bestselling author of *Strong Fathers, Strong Daughters: Ten Secrets Every Father Should Know*

Parenting Ahead

Preparing Now for the Teen Years

Kristen Hatton

New
Growth
Press

newgrowthpress.com

New Growth Press, Greensboro, NC 27401
newgrowthpress.com

Cover Design: Faceout Books, faceoutstudio.com
Interior Typesetting & E-book: Lisa Parnell, lparnellbookservices.com

ISBN 978-1-64507-278-2 (print)
ISBN 978-1-64507-279-9 (ebook)

Library of Congress Cataloging-in-Publication Data on File

Printed in the USA

30 29 28 27 26 25 24 23   1 2 3 4 5

Contents

Foreword

I FIRST MET Kristen Hatton when I was eighteen years old
and she was a mom with three young kids. Her husband, Pete,
led our college campus ministry. For four years, they opened
their home and poured into young adults, and as they did so,
they gave me a front row seat to parenting in the early years. I
looked up to Kristen and how she navigated life as a young wife
and a mom. After graduation, I moved away and soon married
my college sweetheart. I kept up with Kristen through her blogs
and later through social media. Even from afar, I admired how
she intentionally parented and the way they were raising their
children. As the years went by, Blake and I had three kids of our
own.

I was always drawn to the work God was doing in Kristen
and her family. I didn't see a perfect family with perfect kids, or
nice parents who had "good kids" (although they are all lovely
people). I saw a family who lived out the gospel in their home . . .
a family who connected and communicated through the teenage years . . . a family who lived redemptively with one another.
I want that for my family and, because you're reading this, I'm
assuming you want that too.

For me, parenting is one of God's biggest blessings. Even with how much love I have for my own kids—the overwhelming realization is that my heavenly Father loves them even more. What a gift. What a responsibility! I don't want to mess this up. But parenting today tends to feel a little overwhelming. We have so many incredible resources at our fingertips helping us navigate this season the best we can, but sometimes all of the guidance, helpful hints, "do this not that" advice can feel like more of a burden than a blessing.

Lucky for us, Kristen has written *Parenting Ahead*. As I'm coming out of the trenches of babyhood and looking ahead to the tween and teen years, I want guidance on how to be prepared for what the next seasons hold. *Parenting Ahead* is more than a how-to book. It helps parents see all things through gospel lenses. It helps parents focus on the big picture by giving gospel-centered guidance on long-haul parenting.

With her personal and professional experiences, Kristen shares practical examples, helpful scripts, and role plays to teach parents how to proactively parent during one season to prepare for the next. This book is full of ways we can connect and communicate with our kids and create a family culture, but it doesn't leave you feeling burdened—like one more thing to add to your never-ending to-do list. Kristen consistently brings it back to the freedom that only the gospel can give us. Our hope and security are in Christ. We, as tired and overwhelmed parents, can rest in the truth that we can never be perfect parents, we can never have perfect children, but we do have a perfect Savior. Kristen uses her gift of writing to remind parents of this gospel Truth and to encourage and guide us through these child-rearing years.

— Megan Michelson
Birds & Bees

Introduction

IN 2017 I wrote a blog post entitled "8 Things Parents Can Do Now to Shape the Teen Years Ahead."[1] The post had so much interest that the following week I expanded the post into a mini blog series, *Before the Teen Years*.[2] The popularity of the series confirmed my observation from speaking publicly and personally with parents: parents of younger children are fearful of the teen years ahead and are hungry for tips and guidance.

At the time I wrote those blog pieces, we had a son in middle school, a son in high school, and a daughter in college. We are now empty nesters. We have fully done the teen years! Not perfectly and not without distress, but in living through our kids' teens years we did learn a lot about parenting teens, as well as learning about ourselves and God. Thankfully, I can also tell you, even with some hard times during their teen years, on the other side of this season we enjoy intact, close relationships with each of our three children plus our son-in-law.

It was from my experiences writing and speaking to parents, being a parent, living alongside other parents, and seeing the struggles of parents and teens that I decided to go back to school for my master's in counseling. Now I work as a counselor, primarily seeing teenagers and parents. My goal is to help families connect, communicate, and live redemptively with one another. Sadly, by the time many families land in my office, the disconnection, lack of communication, habitually unhelpful and downright wrong ways of responding to each other, and the missing (and misunderstood) gospel has created much relational hurt and turmoil. I long to help change this—on the front end.

What if from the time our children are young, we laid a gospel foundation, teaching them who Christ is, and then lived the gospel out practically every day in our homes?

What if we modeled humility, confession, and forgiveness?

What if we prioritized faith and family in such a way that these things order our calendars instead of our activities and schedules?

What if connecting with our children was so preeminent that it actually altered the way we communicate and discipline, and the way they receive correction?

What if our commitment to living for the good of each other and the glory of God drove us in such a way that the world's ways don't knock us off our feet?

What we do or don't do in the early years, and all along the way, will affect how the teen years go. That is the reason for this book—to encourage and equip you toward proactive, intentional, Jesus-reliant, long-haul parenting. To help you parent ahead!

But I need to stop right here and offer a disclaimer—there is no fool-proof parenting formula. What I share in this book may help, but there will still be challenges, maybe even some really hard seasons along the way. The truth is we could do everything by the book so to speak and still our children can struggle. At the same time, we can mess up big time and God in his grace can and does still bring our children to know, love, and obey him.

Let this sink in a minute—we can do everything "right" and our kids not act "right," or we can get many things wrong and our kids become God-fearing, productive adults. And actually, of course, we will all get many things wrong. And we all have to depend on God's mercy and grace to protect, help, and save our children.

As important as parents are—and we are their primary shaping influence—we are not God. He is ultimately the shaper of their lives. But he has given us our children as gifts with the responsibility to nurture them in the fear and admonition of the Lord. He asks us to be faithful in our calling as parents to teach them about him and to model the gospel in our lives together. The Scripture is not an instruction manual telling us exactly how to parent, yet through the lens of the gospel we see who Jesus is and why we and our children need to depend on him for faith, forgiveness, and help in our time of need. And if there was ever a "time of need," it is certainly parenting.

You will notice that doctrine is woven throughout this book because theology matters more than you might realize. How we relate to Jesus will influence how we relate to and treat our children. As a counselor I've also integrated into this book evidence-based counseling research that correlates with God's Word. In doing so, by no means do I intend to elevate scientific research above God's Word, but I love how science supports biblical wisdom and truth.

Some of what you read in this book may feel convicting. The temptation may be to beat yourself up or fill you with shame and remorse. I pray not. At times I belabor certain points because, more than anything, I want you to know the grace and love of Jesus for you even when you aren't the perfect parent. And I want you to rest in the hope we have in Jesus, no matter what.

The book is divided into three parts. Part One builds the case for long-range redemptive, hope-filled parenting. Part Two focuses on some pitfalls that deter us from living out the gospel or cause us to lose sight of or forsake long-range redemptive parenting. Finally, Part Three seeks to encourage you with what living redemptively in your home might look like in real time. Mixed in throughout is the gospel of grace and practical application. Again, what is offered here won't prevent or solve every problem, but I pray your hearts and families will be changed as you grow together in the grace and love of Jesus.

Part I:
A Persevering Perspective

PARENTING IS A long-range endeavor, but in our culture of instant results with an added desire for ease, it's easy to grow weary with the day-in-day-out struggle of parenting. As we live with the pressures of raising a family in the twenty-first century (cultural pressures, busy schedules, high-energy, kids who don't always listen or obey), we can get so caught up in the day-to-day of our family lives that we put building a spiritual foundation for our children on the back burner. This section of the book is meant to encourage you to adopt a long-range redemptive parenting approach *today* at whatever parenting stage you are in, and also to encourage you that persevering in doing so is worth it. Trying to persevere in our own strength however is futile. To endure with patience and grace, we ourselves must be rooted in the abundant hope of Jesus, so we start here by exploring exactly what that hope is.

Chapter 1
Hold Fast

By perseverance the snail reached the ark.
— CHARLES SPURGEON

"I don't know how we'll survive the teen years."
"I think I may hide in my room until it's over!"
"Can I just bring you my teenagers?"
I hear comments likes these often. Though said as a joke, I notice the fear that underlies what parents say to me. How about with you? How would you characterize your thoughts about parenting teens?

☐ Dread
☐ Survivor mode
☐ Opportunity
☐ Other _____

It's normal to feel some anxiety about what's ahead; we are human. But the fact that you picked up this book, tells me, regardless of which box you "checked," you desire to parent with intentionality. But even with the best intentions, in daily parenting it is easy to lose sight of our long-term parenting goals. Or we may not be sure what those goals are or even what they *should* be. If this is the case for you, you are not alone.

When I posed the question, "What is your measuring stick for successful parenting?" on social media, the post barely received a response. Why was that such a hard question to answer or respond to? Perhaps because parents are either unsure what they are aiming for, or possibly in this case, out of fear, too hesitant to say *they* might fall short of their own measuring stick. Take a moment to think about what your vision of successful parenting might be.

Parent like a Farmer

Whatever parenting goals you might have, I would encourage you to have a vision for parenting based on patience and perseverance. Consider what James says:

> Be patient, therefore, brothers, until the coming of the Lord. See how the farmer waits for the precious fruit of the earth, being patient about it, until it receives the early and the late rains. You also, be patient. Establish your hearts, for the coming of the Lord is at hand. Do not grumble against one another, brothers, so that you may not be judged; behold, the Judge is standing at the door. As an example of suffering and patience, brothers, take the prophets who spoke in the name of the Lord. Behold, we consider those blessed who remained steadfast. You have heard of the steadfastness of Job, and you have seen the purpose of the Lord, how the Lord is compassionate and merciful. (James 5:7–11)

Did you catch the repetitive use of the word *patient/patience*? It was used three times. In one instance, James connected patience to a farmer and, in another, to Job, the wealthy, upright man whose great trouble is written about in the book of the Bible by his same name. More about him in a minute. But first, let's think about the life of a farmer.

A lot of long, hard work goes into growing crops. This includes preparing the land, fertilizing the soil, and proactively working to prevent pests and disease. When the farmer plants, he must make sure the seeds aren't placed too close together and, after the planting, the farmer must make sure they receive enough nitrogen and water. He must also contend with weeds and, of course, the weather. While he can manage the weeds if he is diligent, there is absolutely nothing he can do about adverse weather conditions—the weather is completely out of his control.

Does that remind you of parenting? It does me. We do have control over many things, especially when our children are younger, but there are also many times when we are not in control and have to depend on God to do what we can't. I don't know about you, but trusting God with my kids is about the hardest thing in the world.

Remaining Steadfast in Parenting Challenges

Speaking of trust, let's go back to Job. His story is one of great suffering and great trust in God. The Bible tells us that he was known to be a righteous and wealthy man with a large family. But in a matter of days, he lost almost everything—ten of his children, his servants, and his livestock. Plus, his physical health was compromised after developing skin sores.

Satan thought that Job's suffering would cause Job to curse God. Job did grow bitter, but he never stopped looking to God, and God never forsook Job. In and through suffering, Job came to know God in a more real way: "I had heard of you . . . but now my eye sees you" (Job 42:5).

Nothing can thwart God's plans as Job came to know all too well. Yet Job placed his trust in God despite his great loss and well before those losses were restored. In the end, despite his very real troubles, Job's trust was not conditional on the circumstances that God had allowed, but simply because of the power and majesty of God himself. Despite his struggles, James calls Job "steadfast." That is a wonderful goal for our parenting, isn't it? To be steadfast in our faith in God despite the ups and downs of our children and to be steadfast in our love for our children despite those same ups and downs.

I don't need to tell you that parenting is hard. Even if we do everything "right," things will not always go according to our plan. We will experience trials and, along with those trials, suffering. It will be tempting to lash out against God and try to control things ourselves. But in and through the journey of parenting, God has *our* sanctification as much in mind as our kids.

What do I mean by this?

God uses parenting to change and grow us in his grace. We will see more of our sin and selfishness. We will be faced with both our desire to control and our inability to do so. We will judge others and then eat our words. We will question God's goodness and our own. At times we will feel like giving up or in. We will be tempted to blame God, our spouse, or others for issues with our kids. When our kids leave the nest, we'll wonder if we did enough. And then we will realize parenting is far from over. That's where I'm at now with young adult children who still need us. At times, their adult-sized trials make me long for the child-sized trials of the earlier years. Through all the parenting stages, I have come to see how God continues to use the hard places of parenting to grow me in dependence on him, in a way that few other things ever would.

Consider again James 5:11, "Behold, we consider those blessed who remained steadfast. You have heard of the steadfastness of Job, and you have seen the purpose of the Lord, how the Lord is compassionate and merciful."

Before any circumstances changed for Job, Job was changed by God.

The Lord is compassionate and merciful not if we are "good" parents and our kids turn out right, though certainly that is his grace, but he is compassionate and merciful to bring us into a relationship with him so that we always find rest in him, no matter what.

What Does "Standing Firm" Mean for Parents?

James's call is to *establish your hearts*. But how can we strengthen our hearts? We feast on Jesus, the Bread of Life, in his Word. When we do, his truth penetrates our soul in such way that his Word serves as a weapon to ward off the lies we say to ourselves and what Satan and this world want us to fall for. This is how the apostle Paul explains the relationship between faith, God's Word, and prayer:

> Stand therefore, having fastened on the belt of truth, and having put on the breastplate of righteousness, and, as shoes for your feet, having put on the readiness given by the gospel of peace. In all circumstances take up the shield of faith, with which you can extinguish all the flaming darts of the evil one; and take the helmet of salvation, and the sword of the Spirit, which is the word of God, praying at all times in the Spirit, with all prayer and supplication. To that end, keep alert with all perseverance making supplication for all the saints. (Ephesians 6:14–18)

Paul tells us to stand firm on the truths of the gospel because life in this world is a battle—a spiritual battle in which Satan's aim is to knock you off your feet and on to the ground. In fact, the Greek word *palē* that Paul uses in Ephesians 6:12 for *struggle*: "For our *struggle* is not against flesh and blood, but against the rulers, against the powers, against the world forces of this darkness, against the spiritual forces of wickedness . . ." (NASB, emphasis added) references the popular ancient sport of Greco-Roman wrestling. His readers would have known the aim of this particular type of wrestling is to get your opponent off his feet. Therefore, as Paul tells us, the armor we need to withstand the battle is defensive.

Each piece of this armor, like a diamond, is a different cut or aspect of the gospel—all things already done by Christ. There is nothing we can do. Christ has done it for us. Our aim then is to rest in Christ's finished work. For instance, to guard our hearts with a "breastplate" is to realize we are covered in Christ's righteousness and to trust God in all circumstances comes from our "shield" of faith. But Satan, crafty as he is, will use all sorts of tactics in all areas of our lives (marriage, parenting, friendships, work) to try to knock us off the truth of the gospel. For this reason, Paul admonishes us to stand on ground already won.

Standing may sound easy, but have you ever stood in one place for a long time? If so, you know what tends to happen—we buckle our knees, we get shaky, maybe light-headed. It's easy to fall when you have to stand for a long time. It takes work to stand upright. But the work is the Spirit's work within us enabling us to endure. Standing is not a one-and-done thing; it is lifelong pursuit.

Now like the farmer patiently plodding along with his future crop in mind, I want you to imagine your children as young adults. Depending on where you are on the parenting journey, that may be hard to fathom. But just as the farmer would be foolish to think he could simply drop seeds in the ground and sit back to wait for a plentiful crop without tending to them, we too would be unwise to think we could stand firm through the season of parenting children under our roof and beyond without gospel armor on. Likewise, for our children to stand they too need equipping with gospel armor. Therefore, we must proactively consider how the gospel should shape our parenting and what we hope to impart to our children.

Even with this goal in mind, staying the course is not easy. The course is long and includes lots of unexpected bumps and turns. Therefore, we must adjust our mindset from one of complacency, survivor mode, or dread to opportunity as Paul Tripp in his book *Age of Opportunity* challenges parents.[1]

My first encounter with this Tripp book written for parents of teens was when my oldest was only three and my second-born a baby. At the time, my husband was an assistant pastor leading a group of parents of teens through the book. Since they met at our house, I sat in with them, mostly so I could get to know the couples in our new church. Little did I know how impactful that book would be on me even with littles. Literally, *Age of Opportunity* set the course for our parenting. I've been recommending the book ever since.

Tripp calls parenting the most important job we will ever have. Through parenting, he says you have the opportunity "to make a contribution that is worth infinitely more than any career or financial accomplishment."[2] Specifically addressing the teen years, Tripp says, "It's a time to jump into the battle and move toward your teenager. A time for engagement, interaction, discussion, and committed relationship. Not a time to let a teenager hide his doubts, fears, and failures, but a time to pursue, love, encourage, teach, forgive, confess, and accept."[3]

But those things don't just happen. Again, like the farmer, steadfast groundwork is required, *even well before the teen years.* That is why I have parents of younger children in mind with this book. What we do when our children are young matters. It sets the foundation.

What an amazing opportunity you have now to help build that foundation for your younger children with biblical principles, boundaries, convictions, and honest conversations that will help them when they face the challenges of adolescence. It is much easier to speak into the lives of teenage and young adult children if we've been doing so all along. If that is the case, there is far greater likelihood that they will not only listen but bear the fruit that has been sown.

This is not to say that if we didn't get parenting all "right" and failed to set boundaries or speak truth that our kids are doomed. By no means! Through the power of the gospel, change is always possible. Therefore, if you already have older children and wish you had done some things differently, do not despair. God is sovereign even over our failures, and he loves our children even more than we do. There are many great resources for parents of teenagers that will encourage and help you to prayerfully consider how to parent in this season of life: Paul Tripp's *Age of Opportunity*, Marty Machowski's *Parenting First Aid,* and Drew Hill's *Alongside*, to name a few (others are listed in appendix B on page 155). Remember that it's never too late to begin parenting with purpose. But for those with younger children, there is no better time than the present to think proactively about your parenting approach and decisions.

Small Decisions with Big Consequences

Let's consider a few of those decisions here because the parenting decisions you make today will have consequences for your children as they grow older. While it may not seem like a big deal to give in to your kids and/or not consistently discipline them when they are young, doing so means that your children are learning that manipulative strategies work to get their way. The longer those patterns continue the more difficult they will be to overcome.

Track with me here: Imagine you are chatting with other parents at a park while the kids are playing. Your child keeps coming over to ask for another snack. Initially you say, "No," but she keeps whining. Finally, you relent so you can continue your conversation in peace.

Now sometimes we really do change our minds about a decision (and that's okay), but it is important to check your heart motive when you do. In this situation, the giving in was not because your child needed another snack to tide her over to dinner, rather, by appeasing her you bought yourself more uninterrupted time with the other parents. Inadvertently, you communicated to your child that whining, begging, nagging, and/or continuing to ask long enough will produce the answer she wants.

With this scenario in mind, let's fast-forward. Your daughter is now in high school (and it really does happen that fast!). The pattern of her beating you down until you give in has continued, only now her "asks" are not as benign as just wanting another snack. Now she wants to go to a coed slumber party. Initially, you say no, but as she has learned successfully to do, she keeps asking, begging, telling you that EVERYONE else is going. While you may want to hold your ground on this issue this time, more often I see parents who, after years of habitually giving in, give in all too easily.

When the pattern is established where your child learns how to get what he or she wants, the teen years will be so much harder than they already are—on both of you.

In the case of the coed slumber party, if she doesn't know that "no means no," you will listen to her whine and complain all week. She will badger you at every turn, trying to pressure you into say yes. She may give you the cold shoulder. Or threaten you with the fact that she's eighteen, about to go to college, and can do whatever she wants (a common response from high school seniors). The week will be spent arguing. You may even feel guilt over wishing away the short time you have left with her at home. At the same time, you fear what college life will be like for her.

Before I go on, I want to again say that God can redeem all things. As parents we will make mistakes. Thankfully God does not hold our sin against us or view us according to our failures, though we may struggle to believe that's not how he sees us. Psalm 103:8–10 tells us that, "The LORD is merciful and gracious, slow to anger and abounding in steadfast love. . . . He does not deal with us according to our sins, nor repay us according to our iniquities." I will continue to emphasize this so you know even if you have reels of parenting fails you wish to rewind, you are not without hope!

Before we talk specifically about hope in the next chapter, let me paint a different picture for you.

Let's go back to the day in the park where you are chatting with parents while the kids play. This time, when your child comes running over for a snack, you say, "No." But a few minutes later she is back asking again. Instead of allowing her to beat you down or continue interrupting, you excuse yourself from the parent conversation and walk a short distance away with your daughter. You remind her that because God asked you to be in charge of her, her continuing to ask after you said no is disobedient. Perhaps she continues to whine and you need to have her sit for a time by herself until she is ready to play without asking again for a snack. After your conversation and possible consequences, you return to the other parents, and she runs back out to happily play for the duration of your time at the park without another word about a snack.

What just happened is so much bigger than a snack, or that one day at the park! With a concerted effort to teach your child early that your word is your word, along with a biblical worldview (which we'll get to), years later when the coed slumber party rolls around, imagine your child never even asking to go. She's already learned that you won't cave. And hopefully, she's also developed her own convictions. From laying a foundation with boundaries and helping her understand biblically the why behind certain things you do or don't allow, she knew that it wouldn't be wise or good for her to go. Believe it or not, a similar scene occurred in our house.

Unknown to me, a coed slumber party had been planned. Another mom called to ask my opinion, to which I told her that I hadn't even heard about it. My lack of awareness was not from my teenager trying to hide plans but because he had already said no himself! In fact, his no and mine made it easier for others to follow suit, resulting in the coed slumber party plans falling apart all together.

This isn't always the case. There have been lots of times I have very much felt like I was swimming upstream alone, which is one reason I am so passionate about parents coming alongside each other for the big stuff and the daily stuff of life. Similar situations to the one described happen all the time in different ways.

Reactive vs. Proactive

Why do we give in to our children's demands? Sometimes we just want peace and quiet. Other times we are afraid of our children's displeasure or anger with us. But when we operate out of survival mode or with dread and fear, we will likely fall into *reactive* parenting instead of *proactive* parenting.

According to the dictionary, acting in a proactive way encompasses identifying and preventing potential problems before they happen.[4] On the contrary, being reactive is responding to problems or situations as they come up without any forethought. Think back to the farmer. Would he be steadfast if he didn't think ahead about how to protect his crops from pests? If he waited to do anything until an invasion had already occurred, his work to eradicate the pests and salvage his crops would be far more difficult and costly. Whereas the farmer in James 5, from the beginning, steadfastly and proactively tended to his crops, believing his work would eventually produce the "precious fruit," and his labor would have been well worth the effort.

Therefore, to be a PROACTIVE parent requires thinking about the following:

- what we do and don't allow and why
- the conversations we want and need to have with our kids

- how we want to respond to our kids
- how we discipline our kids
- what we prioritize as family
- what we hope to impart to them while they are under our roof and how to get there

For the Christian, the gospel should inform all this. When we are not proactive:

- Daily opportunities are missed to shape our kids' hearts with the gospel.
- We get buried in the here and now.
- We are either naive, or bury our heads in the sand.
- Our kids face things before we've thought through or had conversations about them.
- We make snap decisions instead of thoroughly, biblically, prayerfully evaluating them.

My prayer is the rest of this book will encourage you to stay the course or adopt now a long-range, proactive, enduring approach to parenting. It will be hard work. The alternative is even harder.

Questions for Reflection and Discussion:

1. Did this chapter shift your view on raising kids and the teen years ahead? If so, how?
2. Has your tendency as a parent before now been more reactive or proactive?
3. Are there any small decisions you have made that you plan to rethink?
4. How might Satan try to knock you off the gospel specifically in parenting and how do you think that putting on the armor of God is connected to your parenting battle?

Chapter 2
Hope Unfailing

If your hope disappoints you, it is the wrong kind of hope.
You see, hope in God never disappoints, precisely because
it is hope *in God.* This means that hope placed in any
other thing will always end up disappointing.

— PAUL DAVID TRIPP

LET'S CIRCLE BACK to what yardstick you use to measure your parenting. What popped into your mind when I first asked that question? We all have ways to assess how we are doing and they are mostly based on how our children are doing. Formal and informal data often point to happiness, health, and success as three of the biggest hopes parents have for their children's future.[1] These aspirations for our children often become the measuring sticks of successful parenting.

There is nothing wrong with wanting our kids to be happy, healthy, and successful. I would be lying if I said I didn't want those things for my children. But if our hope lies in their happiness, health, and/or success, we will feel anxious, angry, disappointed, insecure, and unhappy any time these ideals are threatened.

Even though I consciously try not to be an overbearing mom, I have to admit that, on occasion, I have come to my children's rescue by rushing a forgotten assignment to school or helping complete an application before a deadline. Often, fear of our kids' unhappiness, adversity, or failure sends us into overdrive trying to manage and control. We will talk in a later chapter about how these measures and other desires become controlling desires that influence our parenting styles and behaviors. But just as building a strong foundation in our homes is vital for our children's physical, emotional, and spiritual development, establishing a foundation of hope is essential to life, not just as a parent, but as believers in the fallen world in which we live.

This chapter may not seem very parenting-focused to you, but knowing why Jesus is our hope and how he sustains us is foundational for us as Christians, as parents, and as the primary spiritual leader of our children. But to move from hope feeling like an empty platitude to becoming your very lifeline, you must get to know the person of Jesus—his work and worth for you as Savior, Redeemer, and Friend—as revealed in God's Word.

Hope Has to Be Based on Something Real

The Bible has a lot to say about hope. Its message is rooted in hope. Beginning in Genesis, Adam and Eve are created to live as image-bearers in God's kingdom under his rule, ruling over his creation. Everything at that time is characterized by righteousness. Adam and Eve have a right relationship with God, with each other, and all of creation. That is until they listen to the voice of a different ruler—the serpent—and throw off God's rule.

Shattering God's image to bear the likeness of the serpent (how crazy is that!), their sinful rebellion led to banishment from God's dwelling place and a death sentence for all humanity. Instead of living in safety and peace inside God's kingdom, they would live subject to Satan in a world where sin and death rule. But in Genesis 3 there is a shocking twist—a promise that reveals the graciousness of God's character. He tells of the "seed" he would send, a Promised One, to render Satan powerless, redeem fallen humanity, and restore righteousness. And through the rest of the Old Testament, we see the unfolding story of two kingdoms, two families, two seeds.

In Genesis 12, we learn through God's promise to bless Abram (his name prior to being changed to Abraham) with a people and a place that the "seed" from Genesis 3 will come from his lineage. From that point on, God's people anticipate with hope the One whom God promised to send as their deliverer. By no means was theirs a perfect faith, far from it! God's people (the Israelites) continuously doubt God. And yet, God remains faithful and steadfast to his promises.

Nowhere is God's steadfast, loyal love clearer than in the book of Exodus, which lays out for us God's pattern for redemption. Under the wrong ruler in the wrong place, God's people are slaves subject to death in Egypt. They cry out to God, and he hears them. God sends Moses as a redeemer to rescue them from slavery and death and bring them to the promised land. Along the way, despite God's mighty hand and constant provision, they rebel. But God never forsakes them.

In Leviticus, Numbers, and Deuteronomy, God's people learn how to live as God's redeemed people through their time wandering in the wilderness for forty years! In Joshua, after conquering God's enemies, they are finally delivered into the promised land. Eventually they are ruled by God's appointed king—King David—a descendant of Abraham. King David wants to build a temple to permanently establish God's dwelling place with them. But God tells David that he is not the one who would establish God's permanent kingdom and everlasting rule. Rather it would be someone from David's seed.

As you see God's story progressively unfolding to involve a plan, light bulbs should be going off. The Old Testament shows us the outworking of God's promise to redeem fallen humanity and restore his kingdom through a Redeemer. The hope of Israel and all humanity enslaved under the rule and reign of the serpent rests in the faithfulness of God to fulfill his promises to Eve, Abraham, and David by raising up their "seed" to crush the serpent. Doing so is the only way the consequences of the fall will be reversed, and God's Kingdom restored—a permanent kingdom this time, where God will dwell with his people forever.

Now fast-forward to the New Testament, the hoped-for Messiah finally arrives, but Jesus's birth and subsequent ministry don't unfold as the people expect. Instead, many are confused, angered even. Jesus doesn't act like the warrior-king they had thought was coming. This unassuming man hangs out with criminals, heals outcasts, and talks oddly about the kingdom of heaven. Surely, he is not *the* king who they had hoped for.

After Jesus's death, even his disciples feel their hopes dashed. But then comes a plot twist to the already unanticipated string of events surrounding Jesus's life and death: Jesus's tomb is found empty! Soon after, Jesus reappears on the road to Damascus to two weary travelers to whom he explains how all the Scriptures point to him. "'O foolish ones, and slow of heart to believe all that the prophets have spoken! Was it not necessary that the Christ should suffer these things and enter into his glory?' And beginning with Moses and all the Prophets, he interpreted to them in all the Scriptures the things concerning himself" (Luke 24:25–27).

God *was* faithful to send his promised "seed," and Jesus perfectly fulfilled all that he came to do.

What does this brief Bible synopsis have to do with hope? Hope has to be based on something real. It can't just be wishing that eventually things will turn out okay. Our hope as Christians and as Christian parents is based on God's real, amazing, and sacrificial love toward us. It is in Jesus's life, death, and resurrection that we see God's heart for us. God did not leave us as outcasts, enslaved in a world broken by sin. Rather, he did the unthinkable in sending his Son to endure all the suffering and hardship of this world. The exact thing we try our hardest to prevent for our kids! But that wasn't the worst of it. Can you ever imagine rejecting your child? That's what God did at the cross. He turned his back on his only Son so that he could bring us into permanent dwelling with him! You've likely heard this, but just let this sink in: our Father God did the unthinkable to the One whom Scripture tells us he was well pleased with, so he could make *you* his child (Matthew 3:17).

Because God brings all who turn to him in faith into his family to live forever with sins forgiven and sorrows forgotten, we are never without hope. As God's dearly loved children, we are forgiven, healed, freed, and made new. Our future is secure— we will be in heaven with our God who loves us and laid down his life for us.

But as humans we struggle to see our daily experiences through the lens of heaven. Our struggles can feel more real than the unseen reality of eternity. Therefore, we must fight to hang on to hope by drawing upon foundational truth. There is a reason that battle imagery is used throughout God's Word. Remember that in Ephesians 6, we are called to put on the armor of God, including the belt of truth (the gospel), breastplate of righteousness (this is Christ's righteousness for us), shield of faith, helmet of salvation, the sword of the Spirit (God's Word), and sandals enabling us to stand firm in God's peace, so we can go to battle against the schemes of Satan. We need all of God's armor because one of Satan's favorite schemes is to convince us that our current circumstances are more certain than God's promises.

How does the truth of God's love and power become more real than our current struggles? I often reflect on three anchors of hope that will stabilize us not just in our parenting, but in all of life. Without these anchors, it's all too easy for discouragement and despair to find a home in our hearts.

Anchors of Hope

1. God Is Faithful

Remember the Israelites? When things didn't go according to their plan or timetable, they were quick to lash out against God. They blamed him for their current situation, accused him of breaking his promises, and leading them into misery. Not just once, but repeatedly. And we are no different. Out of our fear, frustration, impatience, anger, or other emotions, we try to wrangle control just as they did when they fashioned the golden calf (perhaps a gentler image of a god they wanted, a god they thought they could control).[2] And when our efforts fail or conditions worsen, if we're honest, it's God with whom we are most angry.

Look at all I've done for you, God. You owe me.

Why are you not helping me (in the way I have already decided I need help)?

Why are you answering their prayers, and not mine?

Why do so many bad things happen to our family and other people have such perfect lives?

Though our current circumstances may feel more real than what God's Word says is true, God has not forgotten you. Just like with the Israelites in Egyptian captivity, God hears you, he sees you, and he knows you (Exodus 2:23–25). By the very nature of who he is, he will make good on his promises to us. However, he may not answer or act according to our will. We may continue to struggle through really hard times and for far longer than we desire or hope for, for far longer than even seems fair.

A prosperity gospel is a false gospel that would have you believe that if you do what you are supposed to do, God will bless you. This view of how God relates to us is synonymous with monetary prosperity, happiness, well-being, a perfect family, ease, and peace. But the perception that we deserve blessing based on what we do is not in line with the true gospel.

God's promise to us is not a life of ease! According to Scripture, the only thing we deserve is death (Romans 6:23), and we contribute nothing to the abundance of God's mercy and grace in our salvation (Ephesians 2:4–9). By the same token, we can do nothing to lose our salvation. This is the ultimate blessing. As God remained steadfast in his loyal love to the rebellious, idolatrous Israelites, so is he with us too. His Son's life, death, and resurrection on our behalf is his guarantee. Here is how Paul explains this, "He who did not spare his own Son but gave him up for us all, how will he not also with him graciously give us all things?" (Romans 8:32).

We can also be certain, because of Christ's finished work, that the heartache of this world will one day pass away. The end of the story is already written. Jesus came and conquered sin, ensuring victory over Satan. But for a little while (I know it can feel like eternity), we must endure the wilderness and all its trials. But not without a sure hope that our inheritance of the promised glory is coming. God will faithfully deliver.

Even still we are tempted to believe God is absent or doesn't care. I recall during my daughter's high school years crying and asking God to intervene in her struggles with body image that led to an eating disorder and depression. Why wasn't he taking it away when I knew he could? Why did he allow others to thrive without the same cares when every day, every hour I felt like we were under attack?

I'm sure you've had similar thoughts. Maybe your marriage is tough, and you're not sure it will survive, or how you or your kids will survive if it doesn't. Maybe sickness is affecting your family, or you are grieving the loss of a loved one. Maybe your child is riddled with anxiety and nothing you say or do seems to alleviate her fears. Maybe finances are tight, and the needs are many. Maybe your loved one doesn't know the Lord—you long for him to know the truth and live obediently to God, but feel hopeless with how antagonistic he is right now.

Whatever it is for you, it's easy to forget God's faithfulness in the midst of trouble. We may think we don't deserve what we are experiencing based on our "good" behavior and therefore accuse God of being absent. Or we might think that, because of our "bad" behavior, God is punishing and abandoning us. Oh, how Satan loves to capitalize on our faulty thinking to move us into that space where we start to accuse and doubt God. Satan knows if he can lead us to discontent and hopelessness, we are more vulnerable to temptation and sin. We are more apt to place our trust in false sources to fill us in ways nobody or nothing but God can.

We need another word than the voice in our heads. We need the truth of who God is to remind us that he is loving and good, steadfast and faithful. We have this reminder in God's Word: "In the beginning was the Word, and the Word was with God, and the Word was God. He was in the beginning with God. All things were made through him, and without him was not anything made that was made. In him was life, and the life was the light of men. The light shines in the darkness, and the darkness has not overcome it" (John 1:1–5).

Jesus is the Word of God coming off the page. He was with God from the beginning, and he will be with us until the end. He has already defeated Satan and secured our standing before God. No matter what comes our way, we can know, because of Jesus, the Light of the world, that God is good and faithful to us even in times of deep darkness.

Still, we forget and lose hope. Therefore, I encourage you to tuck the Word of God in your heart by memorizing Scripture. There is no better way to rest in God's perfect peace than to saturate our minds with God's Word. Isaiah 26:3 tells us that, "You will keep in perfect peace those whose minds are steadfast, because they trust in you" (NIV).

To get you started I've listed a few verses to help you remember who God is when life feels hard. Again, God's faithfulness to us is seen in Christ, so as you read these verses or find others, focus on the finished work and worth of Christ. He did it all, there is nothing you can do in and of yourself. For example, when we read in Deuteronomy 31:6 to "be strong and courageous," think of the One who was strong and courageous for you. Or, with some of the verses, fix your mind on the One who was perfectly faithful for you. Our hope is in a person. "For all the promises of God find their Yes in him. That is why it is through him that we utter our Amen to God for his glory" (2 Corinthians 1:20).

Take some time to read and memorize one or two of these verses. When your mind and heart are discouraged and hopeless, take just one verse and pray it back to God.

- "Know therefore that the LORD your God is God, the faithful God who keeps covenant and steadfast love with those who love him and keep his commandments, to a thousand generations" (Deuteronomy 7:9).
- "Be strong and courageous. Do not fear or be in dread of them, for it is the LORD your God who goes with you. He will not leave you or forsake you" (Deuteronomy 31:6).
- "The steadfast love of the LORD never ceases; his mercies never come to an end; they are new every morning; great is your faithfulness" (Lamentations 3:22–23).
- "For the word of the LORD is upright, and all his work is done in faithfulness" (Psalm 33:4).
- "Your faithfulness endures to all generations; you have established the earth, and it stands fast" (Psalm 119:90).
- "For I am sure that neither death nor life, nor angels nor rulers, nor things present nor things to come,

nor powers, nor height nor depth, nor anything else in all creation, will be able to separate us from the love of God in Christ Jesus our Lord" (Romans 8:38–39).

- "Let us hold fast the confession of our hope without wavering, for he who promised is faithful" (Hebrews 10:23).

In addition to flooding our minds with Scripture, when you get to the other side of a trial and have seen God's deliverance, make note. It's helpful to find ways to memorialize God's faithfulness as was common in Bible times. For example, the twelve stones stacked on the riverbed after God parted the Jordan River for the Israelites to cross over were a reminder of God's faithfulness (Joshua 4:1–6). Taking this concept, you might paint a rock, create a Christmas ornament, purchase a decorative sign with a certain verse, paint a canvas, even get a tattoo as my daughter got after a hard-fought eating disorder battle. It doesn't matter what you do, the point is to have something visual that you can look upon and remember God's faithfulness in the past. Because as you know, we easily forget. Something else that helps me hang on to hope is writing down blessings that come even in the midst of a storm. Keeping a journal to record the ways God shows up and provides not only helps me focus on God's goodness instead of my present despair but gives me a future reminder when doubt and discontent sneak back in.

2. In Christ We Are Secure

Before God spoke the world into existence, Jesus was with God in heaven, sitting on his throne, basking in all glory and praise. He was in the center of utter perfection—where there is no suffering, no broken relationships, no tears. Only joy and perfect contentment. And yet Jesus willingly left the splendor of heaven to wrap himself in flesh. In the flesh, though a king, Jesus lived a humble, hard life of rejection, misrepresentation, abuse, and attack.

Goodness, here we live trying to grab hold of glory so the world would worship us when Jesus, who had all the glory, shed it for impersonators like us. Likewise, he chose to endure sadness, sickness, and suffering when he could have held on to the eternal bliss of heaven that we try to capture here but can't.

The only way I can even begin to wrap my mind around what Jesus did for us is by thinking about all the times as a mom I wished I could take upon myself whatever hard circumstance one of my children was experiencing. "Let it be me," I've thought and prayed, and I bet you've felt that way too. As parents we would do anything to take pain away from our kids, just as we would do anything to protect them from harm's way. It's a no-brainer—we are driven by our deep love for them.

Jesus came on a rescue mission because of his deep love for the Father and us and because of the Father's deep love for us! Think back to the most familiar verse in all the Bible, one we often recite without letting it really sink in: "For God so loved the world that he gave his only Son" (John 3:16a).

God gave his Son because there was no other way for him to be reconciled to sinners. His standard is absolute perfection, and we fall far short. Christ didn't only have to die for us, he had to first live the perfect life for us. In doing so, he met God's standard of righteousness that we could never attain. Because he did, God counts Jesus's perfect record as ours, as if we did it! That's amazing grace! To think we are seen by God as perfect, holy, and righteous despite our ongoing sin because Jesus delighted to hand over his accomplishment to sinners like us. Therefore, we can be assured that God does not hold our sin against us, but instead smiles upon us.

Do you know God's smile? Or are you living under his supposed frown believing you must be better, do better, get better first?

When you encounter what Paul writes in Galatians 2:20b, "and the life I now live in the flesh I live by faith in the Son of God, who loved me and gave himself for me," I want you to be filled with *hope*. Hope in the reality that, though we still sin and deal with the daily struggles of this broken world, we can live trusting and believing that God delights in us because of Jesus's work and worth.

What this means is that when you mess up, even for the millionth time in the same way, your standing before God does not change. Remember, the Christian life (and your parenting) is not about what you do for God, it is about his finished work for you which means you're free from trying to be your own savior. You don't have to work to earn his love or acceptance. You are called to believe that Jesus loved God perfectly for you. Because this is true even when we fail, we don't have to fear his punishment, rejection, or the withholding of blessing.

If this sounds too good to be true, consider the scene in Exodus 33 when Moses begs God to show his glory to him. The Hebrew word for *glory*, which is *panim*, is interchangeable with *presence* and *face*. Essentially what Moses is asking of God is to see his face.[3] Think about the comfort that comes to scared children when they see Mommy or Daddy's face. Or children who have just been disciplined who need the assurance of their parents' love, which is found by looking into their face and seeing loving eyes and a smile. Moses wants to see God's face, to be reassured of God's favor after so much disobedience from the people he leads. God does reassure Moses of his favor by responding that he would make all his goodness pass before him, but still he is not allowed to see God's face (Exodus 33:12–23).

Fast-forward to the time of Jesus. "For God, who said, 'Let light shine out of darkness,' has shone in our hearts to give the light of the knowledge of the glory of God *in the face* of Jesus Christ" (2 Corinthians 4:6, emphasis added). Moses only got God's back, but in Jesus, we can look full in God's face. We have his favor; it's a guarantee of "no more condemnation" (Romans 8:1). There is no reason for shame or hesitation in going to God, even in our sin.

Therefore, when you find yourself wallowing in "mom/dad guilt" or beating yourself up for being a "bad parent," fix your eyes on Jesus.

When you see how your failure to discipline has adversely affected your child, fix your eyes on Jesus.

When you have said something that you deeply regret and can't take it back, fix your eyes on Jesus.

When you are filled with remorse over the times you essentially ignored your child because you were consumed with your own agenda or scrolling through social media, fix your eyes on Jesus.

When you are tempted to spiral down into self-condemnation, fix your eyes on Jesus.

In Jesus, we have God's smile. Under his smile we can live as dearly loved children. His love is never-ending and our future inheritance is secure.

3. We Are Being Transformed

I hope that simply reading this third anchor point fills you with hope. For "he who began a good work in you will bring it to completion at the day of Jesus Christ" (Philippians 1:6). You, who are in Christ, will not remain as you are. Yes, we will battle sin until glory, but we will also continue to grow in his likeness. This is the process of sanctification, the putting to death of sin and becoming more like Jesus. Or, as I like to think of sanctification, the process of growing in grace.

Sometimes we see evidence of God's grace at work within us. The fact I can let shoes, clothes, books, paper, and miscellaneous stuff pile up in our common living spaces (even if just for a short time) is evidence of God's grace at work in my life.

In the past, everything had to be in its "home." While there is nothing wrong with the desire for things to be orderly, I was not okay when things were a mess and would grow bitter toward the people in my household who failed to keep my standard of perfection. I still like order and find joy in a picked-up house, but it no longer rules me in the same way.

At other times, we wonder why in the world we are still struggling with the same old things. Shouldn't we be further along by now? Well, here's the deal: we aren't in control; God is. God is over our sanctification process. Therefore, take heart in knowing that your growth or lack thereof is exactly as God intends it to be. And sometimes, as I learned from Barbara Duguid in her book *Extravagant Grace*, sometimes God leaves us in our sin.[4] I know that might be hard to swallow, I mean why would he do that if he hates sin? But the older I've gotten and the longer I've sinned, the more I see that it is my sin and struggles that keep me dependent on God and needy for his grace. If I didn't sin or never struggled, I wouldn't need him so much.

But believe it or not, even in our sin, we can be growing in grace. This is because, as we become more aware of the deceitfulness of our hearts, the more we will see our sin. At the same time, the more we come to see his perfection as our righteousness, the more quickly we will go to him and others in our sin. This is grace. Also, it's God's grace that, as we see and hate our sin more, our thanksgiving and praise for what Christ has done for us will grow. You may have heard it said that our view of sin and our view of God will rise and fall proportionally. If we think little of our sin, we will think little of what God did for us. When we think much of our sin, we will think much of what God did.

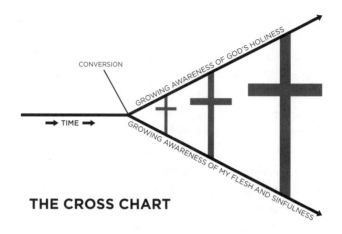

THE CROSS CHART

Used by permission of Serge.

Think with me a minute about what Paul says in 2 Corinthians 3:18, "And we all, with unveiled face, beholding the glory of the Lord, are being transformed into the same image from one degree of glory to another. For this comes from the Lord who is the Spirit."

How does he say we are transformed?

By beholding the glory of the Lord! To gaze upon, observe, see, as *behold* is defined in the dictionary.[5] In other words, it is by setting our eyes on the wonder of who Christ is and what he has done that the Holy Spirit transforms us more and more into his image. Practically speaking, if my tendency has been to blow up at my kids but I begin to deal honestly with what's underneath my anger and see that Christ was never sinfully angry for me, my thankfulness over the grace he shows me increases. At the same time, by beholding him and all that he did for me, little-by-little I begin to show more grace to my children. Maybe I don't blow up so often, or maybe when they get emotional, I am more patient and compassionate toward them. From one degree of glory to another, Jesus begins to transform us. Praise be to God we will not remain static!

There is always hope of change and growth, and if this is true of us, it is also true for our children. But as much as we want to fast-track their change and growth, Jesus is the one in charge of their sanctification too. We get to be instruments—not the physicians.

This is hard for us because we want to control or at least to know the end of the story to help us better trust along the way. But there is something else important to know about sanctification—it is never just about one person. My process of growing in grace—how fast or slow, up and down it is—impacts my husband and kids and other people in my life as well. The same is true for all of us. For instance, my daughter's struggles were not just about her. Through the trial, God was working good in her, growing her in his likeness, and at the same time, he was using her trial for good in my life. On the other side, neither one of us was left unchanged.

As believers we have a lifetime ahead of us of being transformed. There is no short-cut to perfection, only in glory will we be rid of our sin and struggles. As parents I hope this helps you see that there are no formulas to follow. Sure, there is good advice, and as this book proposes, there are things we can do to aid in the spiritual development of our children, but our hope as parents is not that our children will be changed by our following a how-to list. Of course, God calls us to be faithful. Of course, he helps us to be faithful. But our hope is not in our faithfulness, but in Jesus's faithfulness to us.

Jesus is "the founder and perfecter of our faith, who for the joy that was set before him endured the cross, despising the shame, and is seated at the right hand of the throne of God" (Hebrews 12:2). Therefore, as the preceding verse states, "let us run with endurance the race that is set before us, looking to Jesus" (Hebrews 12:1). When we stumble and fail (which we will), and when our kids stumble and fail (which they will), may the enduring reality of Jesus's steadfast love help us rest knowing that God still smiles upon us and loves our children even more than we do.

Though I've heard and sung "Amazing Grace" a million times, one particular Sunday at church I was struck by this line from the familiar hymn: "The Lord has promised good to me. His word my hope secures, He will my shield and portion be as long as life endures."[6] That's it, my prayer for this book is that it would encourage you to root yourself in the truth of God's Word, so you grasp a little more—and a little deeper—who he is for you and your children. And in knowing him better, he would be your life, your hope, your shield, and your portion. That you would trust in his goodness and faithfulness to you even when your circumstances tell a different story.

Questions for Reflection and Discussion:

1. What are the lies of Satan you tend to believe when life is hard?
2. Where have you seen God's faithfulness to you?
3. How do these anchors of hope comfort or challenge you?
4. What are some verses that you could add to the ones included in this chapter? Pick two or more and write them out here.

Part II:
Parenting Pitfalls

PART II IS designed to help us further evaluate our own hearts before we move to shepherding our children's. We will look at three specific areas that cause us to lose sight of or forsake a long-range, redemptive parenting approach. Those areas include worshipping something/anything besides God, believing the lies we hear in our world, and not having a theology of suffering. If any of this doesn't make sense to you right now, don't worry; we will unpack what each one means and how it affects our parenting. Also, a parenting self-assessment has been included as an end of a chapter exercise to aid in expanding our self-awareness as we consider these different areas.

Chapter 3
Parenting Styles and Unintended Results

Kids being raised today have been called the fragile generation.
The children are protected from hardship and pain is prevented.
We shield them from disappointment. We guard them
from discomfort. We hover over homework to fend off failure. We
are poised to pounce if they sit on the bench.
We rescue, we blame, and we excuse.

— LORI WILDENBERG

WHEN MY OLDEST child was a high school senior, I did not realize how closed off she had become toward me. Yes, I knew I drove her crazy with all my reminders of things she needed to take care of. Even I felt like a broken record at times. But when I walked by her room and saw her laying around watching Netflix and on her phone with her friends, *and* I knew how much she had to do, my reminders seemed necessary. Also necessary, so I thought, was the "need" to circle back around later, sometimes just an hour later, to check on her progress—or remind her again to get busy! The solution to the stress and anxiety she complained of seemed simple to me: stop procrastinating!

Eventually my daughter shared how my "nagging" (let's just call it what it is) only served to increase her anxiety, not free her from it. Instead of helping her get going, my nagging was further paralyzing her. She feared what my words communicated to her must be true—I didn't think she could manage her life at college without me. Certainly, I did not think this was true. However, it took a friend drawing an illustration before I could see how my habits of "helpfulness" were suffocating her. My gracious friend then gently encouraged me to stay outside of her bubble unless invited in. Her exact words, I believe, were, "Stop popping her bubble!" Her words opened my eyes to the truth that my nagging was doing the opposite of encouraging her; instead it was provoking her. The very thing that Paul warns parents not to do (Colossians 3:21). No wonder she felt so beaten down.

This is hard for us parents, isn't it? We believe good parents are supposed to "help" their kids. As with me and my on-the-way-to-college daughter, our reason for inserting ourselves is likely the simple desire to prevent unnecessary trouble and to help our kids be successful. But could it be that mixed in with our good intentions, the measuring sticks of their happiness and success are guiding our behavior?

While our intervening may—in the short run—assist in securing our "hopes" for our children, in the long game of life our kids are negatively impacted. Interestingly, as different as helicopter parenting is to hands-off permissive parenting, kids with both types of parents experience many of the same adverse outcomes. So, before we move into analyzing our own motives, or the root beneath why *we* do what we do, let's take a closer look at two pervasive parenting styles and the effects of each on our kids. I will refer to what is often described as helicopter parenting as *overparenting* and permissive parenting as *under-parenting*.

Overparenting

Parents in this category tend to be warm, supportive, and responsive.[1] These are undeniably positive qualities that enable children to thrive. But when these are coupled with a high level of control, parents exhibit too much responsiveness and overinvolvement for what is appropriate for their child's age. Consequently, children are given little opportunity to develop autonomy. Over the years this type of parenting may include things like:

- Being overinvolved in your child's social life, e.g., calling the parent of the girl who didn't invite your daughter to her party.
- Being overinvolved in "defending" your child, e.g., asking the school principal to address the teen who gave your teen a dirty look; going to social media to publicly build your case against the teacher, coach, business who "wronged" your child.
- Being overinvolved in your child's day-to-day athletics or schooling, e.g., demanding the coach play your son or a teacher give your child an assignment redo or deadline extension.
- Being overly restrictive, e.g., trying to keep your child from all infiltrations of the "world" (I'll elaborate on this later as there is a lot of room for differences here).
- Being overly protective, e.g., trying to anticipate every possible safety issue your child may encounter. (Please hear me: it is our job to keep our kids safe but preventing our child from playing soccer because he might get hurt or demanding the city park cover the playground in foam to keep our kids from a bruised knee if they fall are examples that would qualify as excessive intervention.)

If we don't keep ourselves in check, over time, we might become the parents who reach out on behalf of their college kid to question a professor about a grade and intervene in their young adult children's job interviews! I know this sounds absurd, but these things really do happen. Such behavior follows the pattern formed from many years of intrusiveness.

There are smaller, daily occurrences that fall under the overparenting category too. Doing things for your children they should be doing for themselves including, micromanaging homework, tying shoes, making their bed, and then continuing to do for your teen things they are able to do on their own, like make lunches, do the laundry, schedule appointments, and talk to waiters or sales associates. Now you may be thinking, *Well, I do the laundry, what's wrong with that?* For the most part, I do too. But when my youngest was in high school, there were times when he needed something washed, not on a regular laundry day, when I had other things going on. Rather than me rearranging to accommodate his last-minute need, how much better for me to teach him how to do it himself.

The Result of Overparenting

One of the primary problems that stems from overparenting is that our kids don't learn how to navigate circumstances, challenges, and conflict for themselves. Instead of troubleshooting alongside our kids so they learn how to handle things on their own, we take charge, leaving them ill-equipped, insecure, and dependent on us. To a large degree, the rise in college students who feel stressed out and anxious is attributed to the underdevelopment of coping skills and self-efficacy because so many parents have made it a habit to always step in.[2] Furthermore, these young adults exhibit more depressive symptoms and an overall dissatisfaction with life. The very things a parents' control is meant to help their children attain—happiness and success—are the very things these kids lack!

Other implications of overparenting show up in our kids as entitlement and narcissistic traits. Grandiose behaviors, often displayed through dominating extroversion and arrogance, are commonly associated with narcissism. But there is another type of narcissism, the vulnerable narcissist who presents with low self-esteem, anxiety, and depression. These traits are more often seen in someone who has been overparented. However, like the more easily recognized narcissist, both types of narcissists feel entitled to special treatment. Young adults who have grown up with a parent's excessive involvement are accustomed to the world being all about them. Their parents have always been there to meet their every need, resolve every difficulty, and eliminate any roadblock that threatens their well-being. Out in the world, on their own without everyone catering to them, these overparented young adults keep demanding attention from a world that is not that interested.

When children don't learn to deal with life's difficulties and their own failures, they become more dependent on others for their sense of self and worth. As believers in Christ, our worth is secure in him, and yet our sin nature leads us to continue struggling to rest in our infinite, God-given worth. For this reason, we try to attach our identity to false sources or worth—things like our achievements, appearance, wealth, our kids' successes, popularity, others' opinions, and more—to feel good about ourselves or feel our worth. For the young adult, who has not been given the opportunity to become independent, the sinful seeking to know their worth is intensified. Just consider how insecurity and the feeling of being incapable might lead an individual to be hypersensitive to criticism and, in turn, crave special treatment. Is it any wonder this person looks for constant affirmation from others to feel better about him or herself?

While I hear moms joke about being helicopter parents, the result is no laughing matter. If you are concerned that you might be on that path, remember there is a reason we looked first at the hope we have in Jesus. But how this book differs from secular books on the perils of helicopter parenting is that we are going to look at why we are bent toward control. Only then can we repent and ask for Jesus's help to calm our over-anxious, controlling hearts. But first, under-parenting.

Under-Parenting

The term *under-parenting* sounds like it would be a parenting style that no "good" parent would fall into. But my use of this term does not refer to neglectful or uninvolved parents. I am also not using the term, as some do, as an antonym to overparenting which encourages parents to give up the overinvolvement and micromanaging of overparenting. Certainly, under-parenting in that context has it merits. But for the purposes of this book, under-parenting refers to a permissiveness exhibited through failure to exert parental authority, set and enforce limits, and overall abdicate our job of shepherding kids.

Like parents who tend toward over-controlling involvement because they want good things for their child, the under-parenting parent is also warm and responsive because they too want good things for their child. However, their desire for the kids to be happy and for them to have a good relationship results in giving their kids what they want. Examples of under-parenting over the years might include:

- Giving children the freedom to do as they please by setting few or no limits and household rules.
- Doling out money, material goods, and experiences regardless of financial means, such as freely handing out money for social plans so your child isn't left out.³
- Ignoring unruly behavior, for example in a restaurant when a child is disrupting other diners.
- Believing your children without question, such as their claim they didn't do something (that they actually did) and casting blame on someone else.

- Making excuses for your children, such as justifying why they did or didn't do something they should/ shouldn't have.

A belief behind this permissive or indulgent style of parenting is that happy children lead to conflict-free, happy households and good parent-child relationships. Who can blame these parents? That sounds like something we would all like.

Also similar to overparenting, under-parenting begins in a rather benign way. I shared the hypothetical story in chapter 1 of the parent at the park who gave into her child's whining for a snack. As an isolated event, this situation doesn't appear to be any big deal, but after years of indulging a child's every whim, the unwillingness to say no or impose limits on behavior and choices leaves these children vulnerable to entitled thinking. All because we want our kids to be happy, to not miss out, and to think of us as their best friends.

The Result of Under-Parenting

Contrary to our "good" desires that lead to over or under-parenting, children who grow up in either type of home are both prone to anxiety, depression, low self-efficacy, and inadequate coping skills as young adults. Furthermore, a lack of self-control, low perseverance, feeling helpless and becoming easily frustrated are more apt to develop when a mother is materialistically or relationally indulgent with a child.[4] And in the case of separated or divorced parents, when a mother or father emotionally copes by catering to the kids, adolescents become even more vulnerable to the adverse effects of under-parenting.[5]

Research also shows that under-parented adolescents are more prone to outwardly sinful behavioral issues, such as drinking, substance use, sexual promiscuity, and criminal activity.[6] While other adolescents can find themselves on destructive paths with these same behaviors, children accustomed to doing or receiving whatever makes them happy without limits or boundaries are, in a sense, handed over to lifestyles of over-indulgence, excess, and entitlement.

There is much talk today about entitled kids, but do we see how we contribute? When we cater to special treatment and the belief that they have a right to do what they want when they want, we spoon-feed a self-centered, deserving attitude. This is especially visible in upper middle-class homes where kids expect certain designer labels, vacations, and other privileges. But certainly, entitlement is not limited to these households or to this form. One way you might not have thought about entitlement showing up is in the high percentage of young adult males indicted in sexual assault cases on college campuses.[7] According to one journal article, "these youth are more likely to develop expectations that their needs take priority over the needs or concerns of others and a desire for immediate need gratification."[8] Entitlement is identified as a major factor leading young men to believe they deserve sexual pleasure without the consent of the other person. Of course, this is not the only factor, but the entitlement leading to sexual assault is evidenced in under-parented children as well as overparented children. As discussed previously, when a child grows up in the center of their parents' world with everything done for them, they come to expect that they should get what they want when they want it.

These adverse outcomes are hard to take in and certainly not what we imagine will be the result of what we think of as helping our children. But the adverse outcomes are not limited to our children—they also affect us. Just as similar outcomes in under-parented and overparented adolescents have been noted, similarities are evidenced in both types of parents. Stress, anxiety, depression, and overall negative well-being characterize both.[9] I know none of us would deliberately bring more stress into our lives! And certainly, we don't want to feel depressed or have our children depressed. Yet when we veer toward overparenting or under-parenting, we bring it all on.

Can You Be Under-Parenting and Overparenting at the Same Time?

You may be confused about whether you are under or overparenting because you can see yourself falling into both categories. Let me assure you, you are not alone. Ironically, swinging back and forth between the two is not uncommon. In certain areas, perhaps with our children's study habits and grades, we may be all-hands-on-deck, but in other areas, maybe monitoring our children's social media apps or in initiating conversations about pornography and sex, we fail to deal with these things at all. The inconsistency of harping on certain issues and completely ignoring others actually points to something deeper. What is it we value most? Or what is it we value most in the moment? What is it we fear? Or fear so much we would rather ignore it? As we unpack what's beneath our parenting styles, tendencies, and decisions, the hope is that we will grow in self-awareness and in understanding what drives our parenting choices.

What Is Beneath Our Over- and Under-Parenting?

On the surface, many of our actions seem innocently well-intended—we want our kids to be happy, and we want to be happy too. But there is more going on in our hearts. For example, I can't just chalk up my nagging to the good intention of trying to help my daughter. It's true that I wanted to prevent trouble and secure success for her, but also at play was my desire for control and my lack of faith in God's provision for my daughter. Functionally I was trying to be God, believing I knew best. This is what I had to repent of (turn away from and ask God for forgiveness for) and then turn toward God for his help to trust him with my daughter and her future.

44

For change and growth to take place, not just in our parenting behaviors, but in all areas of our lives, we must get to the root cause underneath why we do what we do. This isn't easy for any of us! Naturally we don't like to see our sin. But when, through the work of the Holy Spirit in our lives, our sin is exposed that is a great good because, in seeing our sin rightly, we see more of our need for Jesus. In those moments we can see clearly how much we need the forgiveness of sins and how much we need the help of the Spirit of Christ if we are to turn from our sin toward Jesus. It is in knowing our need for Jesus that we learn to live in greater dependence on him. When our sin is exposed, it doesn't mean we are a bad Christian; it means we are a Christian who needs forgiveness and help from Jesus, as we all do!

Instead of the usual end of a chapter questions, I have included in appendix A on page 151 a parenting assessment as a tool to help you discover what is beneath your parenting tendencies. The assessment seeks to identify strengths, but will likely also point to some idols (those things we make more important than loving God and loving people). I will explain more of what I mean by idolatry in chapter 4, and we will discuss in detail some common idols and false identities we as parents tend to latch on to. You may discover some things through the assessment that you don't like, but I hope that instead of feeling condemnation, you see any revelation of sin to be God's sweet mercy to you and your family. There is always hope with Jesus because with him there is forgiveness. I also hope you find this knowledge helpful as we continue moving through Part II and onto Part III in this book.

Before you flip to the assessment, a few things you should first know:

- This assessment has not been used for scientific, evidence-based research; however, some questions in the assessment are modeled after questions in other assessments used by licensed professionals for parenting research.[10]

- Some questions seek to uncover patterns of over-parenting or under-parenting. Other questions are related to constructs such as values, redemptive living, building connection, and setting limits.
- Unlike most assessments, there is no scoring or classifying you in any way at the end. That may disappoint some of you, but the intent is not to grade you on how "good" or "bad" your parenting is. Rather, I hope the information will be useful as we dig beneath our behavior to evaluate our heart motives, idols, and false beliefs in light of God's Word.

After taking the assessment and processing the content in this book, you may find it helpful to talk through what you discover about yourself with your spouse, a trusted friend, a small group, a pastor, or a counselor. Choose someone who you can be vulnerable with or who can walk alongside you in real life. This can be a tremendous help in our transformation journey from "one degree of glory to another" (2 Corinthians 3:18).

Questions for Reflection and Discussion:

Turn to appendix A on page 151 to take the parenting assessment and answer the questions. You may want to use a pencil if it is something you would like to retake at another time or have your spouse also do. Upon completion, go on to read chapter 4 about idols and how they affect our parenting.

Chapter 4
Idols—What Are They Good For?

The true god of your heart is what your thoughts effortlessly go to when there is nothing else demanding your attention.

— TIM KELLER

What Is an Idol?

The concept of idolatry may or may not be familiar to you, so let's make sure we have the same understanding of what the words *idol* and *idolatry* mean. Unlike the Israelites bowing down to worship a golden calf or carved image of wood or stone, in our culture an idol is not typically a statue. However, today's idols are similar to the idols in ancient biblical times in that they are still substitutes for God. Quite simply, an idol is whatever rules our hearts, whatever we worship. Pastor Tim Keller says that an idol is, "anything more important to you than God... anything you seek to give you what only God can give."[1]

For some of us what is most important to us—even before God—are things like our appearance, accomplishments, or reputation. Or what we hold most precious might be our wealth, education, career, talent, home, community, or vacation. It could also be a relationship, perhaps with our spouse, a friend, and, maybe most often, with our children. An idol can also be our desire for safety, need for order, or drive toward perfectionism.

The list is endless. And at any given moment a new idol can pop up, which means we don't have just one idol. We may be prone to a particular idol, but as John Calvin wrote in his Institutes, "the human heart is a perpetual idol-factory."[2] Therefore, we are likely to have an idol of the day, even an idol of the moment, seeking to take control of our heart.

Let's take for example the time I sat in the school auditorium waiting for my child's school program to begin. In walked another mom who instantly caused me to bristle. I saw the way she confidently walked in the room, how beautifully she was dressed, and how flawless her skin was. Immediately I was full of self-hate. *Why did I wear this? I look so frumpy, and goodness, the grays surrounding my forehead just frame my wrinkles even more.* Do you see what just happened? I went from content to self-consumed in an instant. Forgetting my security and worth in Christ, a complete makeover became my functional savior of the moment.

As ridiculous as worshipping a statue of a cow sounds, our idols can be pretty crazy too. When Pinterest first became a thing, I remember every mom scouring it for the cutest, most creative treats to take for a class party or baby shower. At that time, it was a new phenomenon to look to the perfect cupcake (of all things) to give us worth. On the flip side, that perfect cupcake presented by one mom became the standard to which another mom believed she failed to measure up. While in one sense the cupcake was an idol, as with the golden calf, underneath is something even deeper still.

What was *it* that these moms believed the cupcake would give them? (Or insert whatever else you might measure your worth with in place of cupcakes.) One answer might be the status of "good mom," but we can go even further to see that the idol underneath the idol is not just to be a good mom, but the desire to be viewed highly by others. In other words, we want to be found worthy. We want to be adored, looked up to, and praised.

We can even say (if we are brutally honest with ourselves) that we want to be elevated to a god-like status in the eyes of others.

Isn't this (at least some of the time) why we post what we post on social media? We broadcast to the world when our child gets student of the month or some other award because we've attached our identity to our child's success. (Not always—only you and God know your motive.) But often we do feed off the praise for our child and feel better or more worthy as a parent. But these things can't satisfy. We will always need more, right? Usher in our next humble-brag post!

From these examples I hope you see how whatever drives our behaviors, habits, and tendencies points to our functional god. For whatever we trust in, hope in, bank on, or must have points to our idol. If you are unsure, a good litmus test for evaluating idols is using Paul Tripp's open palm or closed fist analogy.[3] We can know when a desire has been elevated to idol status when we metaphorically close our fist tight around *it*. Whatever the *it* of the moment is, we do everything in our power to obtain or hang on to it. On the other hand, a desire held loosely as if in an open palm does not exert control over us. It is simply a desire, and if it goes unmet we might feel sad or discouraged, but we won't be devastated.

Another "test" you can use to evaluate what you treasure above God is to take inventory of what occupies your mind over the course of a day or week to see what your mind drifts to most often. Or you might evaluate your emotions. Why did you get so upset when you weren't acknowledged? Why did you feel so jealous? Why did you scream at your kids? What does the anger point to? These are all good questions to ask yourself to help identify the idols ruling your heart.

Parenting Idols

Defining idols broadly helps us to understand that idols can run the gamut of all things, big and small, tangible and intangible.

How might treasuring something above God impact our parenting? There are some specific desires that we frequently elevate to idol status that drive our overparenting and under-parenting tendencies. I know from personal experience that it's hard to uncover what we are worshipping instead of God, but having our sin exposed is good and necessary. God already knows what is in our hearts, and he doesn't love us any less because of it. His smile remains, his acceptance never wavers. We are also all in the same boat. None of us are exempt from sinful idolatry so I'll kick this list off by going first with an idol that frequently hijacks my heart and mind.

Control

Since the essence of idolatry is trying to throw off God's rule and reign to seek after what we think will fill us, we can see why wanting control above all else is the epitome of idolatry. When we live as if we know better than God how our lives should run and what will satisfy, then we have put ourselves in the place of God. Isn't this the age-old story that started in the garden with Adam and Eve? All it took was Satan's whispering lie that God was withholding good from Adam and Eve. And Eve swung into action, taking things under her own control. We've been doing the same ever since.

While I was writing this chapter, our youngest was playing his senior season of football. Leading up to the season, he spent the summer attending various college football recruiting camps and was on the radar screen of several Division I coaches. All he needed was a successful senior season. But when the time came, his high school coach didn't use him as the secret weapon that a 6'5" tight end can be to make big plays. Instead, he used him primarily for blocking. Every game my husband and I came home frustrated, as did our son. I couldn't stand it. I felt like my son was being robbed of his future. I was ready to take control. An email to the coach, a meeting, a passive-aggressive blog post, I had all sorts of ideas I was ready to implement until my football-loving husband gently reminded me that God was on his throne. God did not need me to intervene. Our high school coaching problem was not news to God. Rather, he had even ordained who our coach was and the school our son attended. And if our son was meant to play college ball, God would work that out too—without my "help."

As it turned out, we see now that God was not absent from our son's senior season but allowed what was happening to keep him from playing college ball. While we will never know exactly why, we trust God's provision for our son is better than what we thought best. Arriving to this place of acceptance was not easy. Not at all.

I imagine, like this situation was for me, you too sometimes find it really hard to believe God's control is best and he will work things out. What if God's plan isn't to our liking? Can we take that chance? It feels especially hard to trust God with our kids, which makes the idol of control particularly enslaving for parents. If we are honest, we think we know better than God, so we go to work asserting our control in attempt to secure what we think is best.

Often, interwoven in *our* plans is evidence of other idols. Safety? Happiness? Success? Other people's opinions? Do these strike a bell? We want to ensure our kids' safety. We want to secure our kids' happiness. We want to guarantee our kids' success. We want others to think highly of our kids and us as parents. We act as if our life depends on it.

Control coupled with safety really gets me. While normally not an obsessive worrier, when it comes to my kids and driving, especially late at night or on the highway, I am a wreck (pun intended!). Obviously, it is normal for a parent to be concerned for their child's safety, and idolatrous control is not always the issue. But if I become so obsessed with monitoring every move my kids make on my phone's tracking app, or I never allow them to drive after dark, on the highway, or drive at all, my need for control would be ruling me and hindering them.

For those prone to overparenting, control may top your list of idols as it does for me. Controlling to ensure their safety may look like not allowing your child to climb up the tall slide, play a contact sport, or sheltering your child with the assumption that if you can control your child's environment all will be well.

Controlling to secure their happiness may look like calling another parent if your child wasn't invited to a slumber party or intervening with a coach to make sure your child gets the playing time they deserve.

Controlling to guarantee their success may look like running the forgotten assignment up to school instead of letting a child suffer the consequences. If it is in our control to keep them from getting a bad grade, then we justify that is the better option.

Controlling what other people think about us and our kids may look like law-driven discipline where we care more about behavioral modification than heart-change (we'll talk more about this in Part III). The parent who tends to under-parent is not exempt from control. Control for them (or you) may look like trying to secure your kids' happiness with material goods and fun experiences or never imposing boundaries or discipline.

Control manifests itself in many ways. When we find ourselves clenching our fists around something to ensure things go our way or our kids' way, let that alert us to our need for Jesus. Ask him to help you trust him with all your heart and not lean on your own understanding or self (Proverbs 3:5). Specifically ask him to help you trust him with your kids.

Throughout my children's lives and still today, there are times I struggle to remember and believe that God loves my children even more than I do. My fears and unmet desires for my kids get the best of me and I worry about what God may take them through or leave them in. Therefore, I find in parenting the need for praying for them out of a posture of constant surrender.

My daily prayers for them include, "not my will but yours, Lord." In doing so there are days I feel his peace, but still other days I just can't seem to "let go." However, when I look back over all my years of parenting, I see how the Lord has grown me in his grace in that I more quickly and more frequently turn to him in prayer and find comfort in his truth. This is what it means to live in greater dependence on him, which happens to be one of God's key purposes for us in our parenting journeys.

Comfort/Peace

There is nothing wrong with wanting peace and quiet; we all need downtime and rest. But when we demand comfort or peace at all costs, they too become disordered desires. My husband tells the story about sitting down on a Saturday to watch his college alma mater play football. He is a fanatic, I might add, and he will even admit that Penn State football is an idol for him. Our sons, who were little at the time, had been playing together nicely all morning, but as if perfectly timed to the kick-off, they started fighting. My husband yelled at them to "knock it off"; when they didn't stop, he erupted in anger. The last thing he wanted to do during the much-anticipated football game was deal with disciplining. This was before you could pause the TV! His emotional response was evidence that his desire for comfort had been elevated to idol status.

Of course, my husband is not alone. My desire for peace and comfort looks like me sitting in my chair after a busy day mindlessly scrolling social media or catching up on emails. If my children tell me something then, it's easy for me to dismiss them and miss an opportunity for connection. For some, seeking comfort may look like disappearing to a bedroom to do your own thing, pouring another glass of wine, engaging in your own personal hobbies without regard for the families' best interest, or Moms' Nights Out to the extent that you are regularly leaving your kids in the care of your spouse or babysitter. There is nothing wrong with these things in and of themselves, and enjoying them can actually fill us so we have more to give to our kids. But we must evaluate our hearts to face squarely the frequency and reason for our escapes or the unreasonable demand for them.

Another way we can live for the idol of peace is in the failure to tell our children *no* or set boundaries for them. Are we afraid to rock the peace? Would we rather not stir up conflict or discipline at all because that will disrupt everyone getting along or prolong us from doing what we want? Do we go overboard in catering to our kids to maintain a happy, peaceful household?

For those inclined toward under-parenting, this may hit a nerve. But idols are *false* gods for a reason—they can't deliver! The temporary peace you may gain in avoiding conflict or discipline will most likely produce greater trouble later. For Proverbs 19:18 says, "Discipline your children, for in that there is hope; do not be a willing party to their death" (NIV). In other words, failing to discipline harms them, and can lead to much sorrow. It is worth the discomfort now.

If (or when) you identify in yourself the inordinate demand for peace and comfort, pray that God would enable you to "give up [your]self and [your] own desires" (Mark 8:34 NLV) and "count others more significant" (Philippians 2:3). As humans with an inward bent toward self, this is unnatural to us. We need God's help. And perhaps the help of others too. When we bring our idolatrous sin struggles to light and share with a spouse, a friend, or maybe a small group, they can pray with and for us, and encourage us in the truth. Of course, Satan would love for us not to confess since we are more vulnerable when we are isolated and keep things hidden. But when we can turn to our spouse or send a quick text to a friend to pray for us in the moment we are tempted, their prayers and support can become the very means God uses to help us overcome the desire for our own comfort to rule.

Success (Ours and Our Kids)

As with other idols, success is not a wrong desire, but making it more important than love for God and people and trying to secure success at all costs certainly is. To unpack why success is so important to us, let's consider the identity we attach to success. What does success do for us? How does it make us feel and look, particularly as parents? For example, when my daughter was a young teen she was involved with theater and had the lead role in several productions. Naturally, I felt happy for her success and how hard she worked. But mixed in with that happiness was my sinful desire for my daughter to be seen as great, which I hoped would reflect well on me too! I was tying my worth to her successful performance. I felt good because she did well. Instead of enjoying her performance and thanking God for how he made her and gifted her, I made it about me. I made an idol out of her performance.

How about you? Looking to our children's academic success, athletic or musical accomplishments, other awards, good behavior, and even popularity to tell us that they are good (and therefore we are good) will always end up leaving us unsatisfied and them feeling pressured. Of course, there are many valid reasons for tutoring, lessons, competitive sports teams, and the like. However, many parents sacrifice things such as family connection and togetherness, church, rest, and money, to give kids a leg up, especially when it comes to sports. While there may be scholarship opportunities and future dreams at stake, from what I've seen, many kids burn out and quit before they graduate from high school. Let's not do these things unthinkingly because it's what everyone around us is doing. Instead let's ask: What are we placing *our* hope in? What do we value most? Where are we seeking identity and teaching our kids to find theirs?

Let's also evaluate the effect of the reverse—the lack of "success." Think about it, you've seen thousands of posts from parents showcasing their kids' accomplishments, but what do we do when our kids go unrecognized, are unsuccessful, or flat-out fail? Certainly, we aren't posting! Likely, we are justifying, excusing, despairing, and maybe hiding. Likely we also feel some strong negative emotions. Why? Because we've forgotten God's smile. Our children's lack of worldly success or notice makes us feel like failures. Their success is tied to our identity. And often, where you find one idol, if you keep digging, you find others too.

How can you tell when your child's success has morphed from something that gives you joy and fills you with thanksgiving to a disordered desire? When success becomes an idol, we think of ourselves and our kids as less than or unworthy when accolades and accomplishment aren't attained. Or, when our kids display certain behaviors publicly, we are filled with shame and lash out. Why? Usually it's because we think that we look like a "bad parent." On the other hand, we see ourselves and our kids as better or more worthy when they achieve in school, sports, performances, and popularity. We see our kids as a reflection of us. So it could also be said that our kids are our idols. We look to their goodness to give us worth. We fear their mistakes, or simply them being average or different, deem us unworthy.

I'm embarrassed to tell you this, but when my first son went to college, I wanted him to pledge a fraternity. Not just any fraternity, but the "good" fraternity with lots of Christian boys. He had no interest. He wanted to plug in to a particular campus ministry. I was grateful that he wanted to get involved with the ministry, but I wanted him to do both. As I expected, people began asking me what fraternity he pledged, and I had to say that he didn't. I feared what other people would think about him, and me, because of his lack of social standing (according to my own warped ideas). But isn't gaining the favor of others exactly what we look for success to bring? Once again, we see how there is never just one idol—there are typically several wrapped up together.

Other's Opinions

Living for the opinions of others is what the Bible calls "fear of man." This is definitely an idol we all struggle with. Let's unpack how it is connected to our parenting. When our daughter was a teenager worried about her appearance, my husband used to say to her, "You are telling me that you care more about what a pimply teenage boy thinks about you than the God of the Universe who created you?" Phrased in that way, we could laugh about the ridiculousness of it. But still, she struggled, and we are no different. Too frequently the opinions of others hold more weight than what God declares true. This often leads to both our overparenting and under-parenting. How does that happen?

Both when we overparent and when we under-parent we are often trying to control how others see us. Both are driven by a fear of man, although the audience varies. For the overparenting parent, this may include things like how we dress our kids, what they are allowed to watch, even what they eat. Why is it so important that our child have on a collared shirt or dress shoes? A bow in her hair? Or even match? Why can't he wear a costume in July to the grocery store? Because we care what others think, specifically we fear their judgment! Or take food, do we restrict sugar or carbs or fast food because our all-organic mom friend may judge us? To our child's later detriment, this very thing can lead to disordered thinking and behavior about eating. Because we see our kids as a reflection of us, we may stifle their creativity, try to get them to fit a certain standard of beauty or accomplishment, and lead them to feel less than when they don't measure up—all so that we can look good to others.

With the fear of man idol, overparenting parents are likely to resort to law-driven discipline. Instead of addressing the heart, which we will talk about in Part III, we focus on quick behavioral modification, so our child looks good in the eyes of others. When our idol is other people, everything is about perception.

Parents prone toward under-parenting can also care about what others think, but who those others are likely differs. *Others* may be their children or children's friends. For instance, parents may allow more freedom to be seen as the fun or "cool parent." With younger children, this may mean letting kids stay up way past their bedtime without media restrictions. With teens this might look like hosting a party and serving alcohol to minors. Or the *others* could be your own child. In an effort to be "besties," you relate to your child more like a peer than a parent.

We can make an idol out of anything; so can our kids. But until we start to spot the idols in our lives, we can't help our children see the false sources they turn to. Evaluating why we do what we do helps us identify our idols and subsequently turn from them. As I've said before, we can't repent of what we don't know. Therefore, again, instead of the traditional end of the chapter discussion questions (though you can use these as a springboard to discussion), I encourage you to take some time to complete the exercise below.

Before you do, let us confess and repent of our sin before God. We will experience great freedom and rest. Keeping our sins hidden and unacknowledged, leads to fear, shame, and doubt, which serves only to compound our struggles. But "there is therefore no condemnation for those who are in Christ Jesus" (Romans 8:1). There is no need to fear and no reason to cover up. He beckons us to "come boldly to the throne of grace" (Hebrews 4:16 NKJV). Your sin does not surprise God. Christ died for us in our sin before we wanted deliverance from it (Romans 5:8). Knowing this acceptance—the smile of God that we've talked about—brings us such joy. I have noticed that my affection for the Lord and desire to live pleasing him has grown the more I've seen my sin, just as the cross chart in chapter 2 illustrates. So rather than feeling that my sin disqualifies me from being loved by God, the acknowledgment of my sin *is* what qualifies me to be a child of God covered in Christ's righteousness!

Questions for Reflection and Discussion:

1. Within the blank space of the "golden calf" illustration, or on separate sheet of paper, write down the idols you are most prone to.[4] They may be ones we've talked about or something else.

2. To the left of the platform elevating the calf, list any behaviors driven by these idols, and to the right of the platform write out what leads you to turn to your false god(s). For example, for my idol of control, I would write to the left "it leads to nagging behavior." To the right, I would write, "when I feel helpless and out of control."

3. Finally, write out a prayer asking God to help you be mindful when these "golden calves" rise up in your heart and to turn from them.

Chapter 5
God's Word vs. the World's

When love is plucked from its biblical context,
and morality defined by personal desires, one is left
with a gospel made in our own image.

— ALISA CHILDERS

TODAY TRUTH IS relative. Gender is fluid. Morality is no longer a common consensus. Bible stories once generally known by many aren't anymore. Convenience is everything—streaming television shows, online shopping, information at our fingertips, and dinner or groceries delivered with a click. Communication is constant—smart phones and social media keep our eyes glued to screens. But interpersonal communication is lacking—smart phones and social media keep us from interacting personally. Mental health struggles are soaring—all of the above plays a part.

With technological advancements, cultural changes, and anti-biblical views coming at us at breakneck speed, we too are being changed. Without sometimes even realizing it, many Christians have bought in to the world's way of thinking and doing. Many anti-biblical views are accepted and embraced by Christians, often without any consideration of how they hold up against God's Word. And I'm not talking solely about hot topic issues, but daily choices and priorities that directly affect family life.

Those unwilling to accept what seems to be the new normal have found it requires swimming upstream, against a strong current. But many Christian parents aren't willing to stand firm against culture, which points right back to idolatry. Whether the idol is the fear of others' opinions, not wanting our child left out, popularity, happiness, or peace, we bend to the surrounding pressure without even a fight. After all, life *is* easier when we give in to the world's way. For other parents, decisions are not so much about giving into the world, but stem from the overall lack of a biblical framework to filter all of life through.

Either way, we can't see straight when we're wearing the wrong glasses. It is time for a new prescription. We need gospel glasses.

Gospel Glasses

Imagine sitting in the examining chair at your eye doctor's looking through an autorefractor machine. For those who are unfamiliar, the computerized autorefractor is used by doctors to measure the refractive error in a patient's eyes. With the patient looking through the machine's lens, the doctor clicks back and forth between two images, each with letters on them, but at different levels of focus.

"This one? Or this one? 1 or 2, 2 or 1?" is what eye doctors commonly say as they click through the series of images. At the end of the procedure, the doctor determines the level of correction needed for the patient to see more clearly.

Without the lens of God's Word, our vision is blurry. Naturally all we can see is through the sin-skewed refraction of our desires and the world around us. We need new lenses in order to see God, ourselves, and the world through the gospel grid we need for parenting. What does that mean?

A gospel grid filters everything through God's Word. But first, we need to understand that God's Word is not meant to be used as an instruction manual or a series of moral stories showing us how to live. God's Word is the unfolding story of the gospel—the story about who Jesus is and why we need him.[1] It is a story that you can think of in four acts, outlined as follows.

Act 1: Creation

Genesis 1 tells us that God created the world and everything in it. Everything was ruled by God. Everything was at peace. As the pinnacle of creation, God made people in his image and in accordance to his pattern of order and hierarchy he gave them authority to rule over his creation and to also fill the world through procreation.

Act 2: Fall

As we briefly looked at in chapter 2, when Adam and Eve took the fruit of the tree prohibited by God, sin entered the world and God's image in humans was broken. Sin turned the world on its head. Instead of people glorifying God and living for the good of others, the rebellious, sinful heart of everyone was turned away from God's rule and toward self. Instead of life forever with God, because of their sins, all people lived under a sentence of death.

Act 3: Redemption

But God had a plan to redeem all of creation and reunite his people with himself. He promised a deliverer—a Redeemer. When Jesus came, he entered our brokenness, pain, and suffering, without ever sinning himself. He lived the perfect, holy, righteous life necessary so he could pay the penalty of death brought on by sin. On the cross he took our place. Only through Jesus can we be united with God. Through him we are cleansed, forgiven, made right, and redeemed.

Act 4: Restoration

One day all will be made new, restored to its created order. Though all is far from right in this world now, on that day of Christ's return, all will be made right. This is our certain hope—guaranteed in Christ.

These four stages of God's story help us understand the Bible and interpret everything going on within us and outside of us in the light of God's story of redemption. Understanding the four stages helps us make sense of our disordered desires, longing for fulfillment, and our need to be made right. It also tells us why our hope is secure. Through this lens, we see why we do what we do and how looking to anything apart from Christ will fail to satisfy or help us (and our children) thrive. It provides the hope we need when what we see currently feels more real than God's promises. It points us to Jesus as our Rescuer.

Therefore, I want us to consider some common phrases, philosophies, and practices of today. Think of these as the images we are looking at through the biblical autorefractor machine. From a worldly lens, these ideas, thoughts, and behaviors are completely fine, popular even. But I want to play the part of the eye doctor by bringing these ideas into clearer focus with a gospel lens.

This One? Or, This One? 1 or 2?

Listed in the table below in the left-hand column are popular worldly platitudes, philosophies, and practices you will likely bump up against in parenting, certainly in life. Some are grouped together because of similarity. The middle column is an evaluation of each after running them through the gospel lens of our biblical autorefractor. Doing so I hope makes clearer why these are counter to God's Word. In the right-hand column we'll look through our gospel glasses to take a closer look at how these worldly sentiments might affect our parenting.

As a disclaimer, this list is not exhaustive, nor is the gospel-side commentary and parenting piece a full assessment of any one topic or all the Scriptures that may relate. Rather, the list and the brief responses are meant to increase your awareness of and help you think biblically about ALL the twisted truths and flat-out garbage that comes our way. Many times, we don't stop to evaluate, but instead simply accept because it sounds good or popular opinion embraces it. Unfortunately, even Christians, including preachers, authors, and other influencers buy in to false truth and consequently contribute to the propagation of lies.

The World's Advice	A Gospel Lens	Applying the Gospel to Everyday Encounters
You do you. You only live once.	We are all created unique and special and shouldn't try to be someone else. However, "you do you" implies more of an unlimited freedom to do or be whoever we want without bounds. From a self-autonomous mindset, we forget the beginning of God's story and ours. God is our creator, authority, and giver of all things. To live as if we are our own boss and can do whatever we desire is to reject God's law and our need of a Savior. We are not our own, rather we are united to Christ and his body with the Holy Spirit indwelling within us. 1 Corinthians 3:16, 23; 1 Corinthians 6:15–17, 19	I often hear teenagers affirm and even encourage their peers' choice to be and do whatever makes them feel good. But Scripture is clear, we are not our own. In Christ, we first belong to him. We are to live to his glory and to the good of others. It's easy for parents to adopt the same perspective. But the truth is that we can only "do you" when we live how God intended for us to—for his glory and as worshippers of him. Helping our children from a young age understand that they flourish in right relationship with the God who made them will help steer them from a self-focused, me alone mentality that gives a free pass to do whatever they want.

The World's Advice	A Gospel Lens	Applying the Gospel to Everyday Encounters
Find your own truth. This is my truth. Let your feelings be your guide.	Jesus declares himself to be "the truth" (John 14:6). Truth is not based on what we think or feel. Truth does not change over time. What was true of God in the beginning is true forever. Since the Garden, man has sought to determine what is good and right, what is true, according to our own eyes. But in the first chapter of John, we learn that Jesus was with God from the beginning and that he is the Word made flesh, the revelation of the truth (John 1:1–3, 14). Jesus says "no one comes to the Father except through me" (John 14:6). Jesus is the truth that sets us free (John 8:32). Any other "truth" leads us astray. Our emotions are not exempt from sin so our feelings as a guide can lead us away from truth.	Disney movies are notorious for promoting the view that we should follow our hearts. But since our hearts are deceitful beyond measure (Jeremiah 17:9), we are prone to give more weight to our feelings of the moment than God's truth. Although in our post-modern culture, truth is considered to be relative, that's not what the Bible teaches us. Helping your children to view God's Word as the absolute truth is foundational (Proverbs 30:5; 2 Timothy 3:16).
You deserve to be happy. God wants you to be happy.	These assertions make happiness the be-all and end-all, an idol. Happiness, in this worldview, is contingent on getting what we want. But when the Bible talks about happiness, it is not based on having all our needs and wants met. Rather happiness comes in finding our joy and contentment in the Lord regardless of circumstances. The idea that we deserve happiness points to entitlement and underneath entitlement is discontentment with God and what he has given us. From a worldly perspective, happiness tends to be what we think life is all about. But in the brokenness of this world, happiness is a gift of grace, a taste of heaven, that will not be perpetually experienced until glory. Matthew 5:6; Luke 12:15; 2 Corinthians 12:10; 1 Timothy 6:6; Hebrews 13:5	Who doesn't want to be happy? It should be no surprise that our children at times play to our emotions in manipulative attempts to get what they want. Rather than always giving in to their asks (and demands), with a long-range parenting approach in mind, we need to consider the implications of instant gratification. Giving them what they ask for and think they need for happiness will only result in more demands and a deep discontentment. True biblical happiness is the byproduct (not the goal) of a life of loving God and people. We would do well to consider what we want most for our kids. If happiness is the goal, entitlement and self-indulgence will be the likely result. But temporal happiness is only that. It is fleeting. A life in Christ is the only thing that can fully satisfy. Therefore, let's help our children learn contentment in all circumstances (Philippians 4:11–13).

The World's Advice	A Gospel Lens	Applying the Gospel to Everyday Encounters
Live your best life now.	This too is a misguided sentiment that is not compatible with living a life honoring to Jesus. The goal of "living your best life now" implies doing whatever makes us happy at all costs. It's the opposite of what Jesus calls us to—denying ourselves, taking up our cross, and following him Matthew 6:19–24; 16:24–26; 22:37–39	Jesus tells us that in this world we will have trouble (John 16:33). Our kids need to know this. This sinful, broken world cannot fully satisfy. Living as if it can satisfy or that we must always be living our best life will leave us deeply disappointed. In parenting we can help our children when they start to compare their lives or circumstances to what others' have by reminding them that life is about more than having what you want right now. Isn't this what so often happens as we scroll through social media? Furthermore, let's challenge what the world calls "your best life," measuring it against what Scripture calls a life worth living. According to God's Word, it is in giving up oneself, serving, loving others that we experience the best of this world (Matthew 10:39; Mark 8:34).
Do what you need to do for you. I can't give to others until I take care of myself.	The Bible calls us to deny ourselves and to live for the good of others. While it is important to take care of ourselves, that can become an idol when we start to demand "me-time" and live selfishly for our own good. Rather, the call of the Christian is self-sacrifice. "For you were called to freedom, brothers. Only do not use your freedom as an opportunity for the flesh, but through love serve one another" (Galatians 5:13) John 3:30; Luke 9:23–25	Our human bent is toward self. Therefore, to help your kids think outside of themselves, you may consider serving as a family—making it a regular part of your family rhythm. Or you may ask older kids to help with younger siblings or any age child to help with age-appropriate chores as a way to serve the family. Along the way, have gospel conversations about what it means to sacrifice for the good of others and not live for self.

The World's Advice	A Gospel Lens	Applying the Gospel to Everyday Encounters
If I'm not hurting anyone, it shouldn't matter what I do.	In the same vein of "You do you" and "I deserve to be happy," we act as if we are autonomous when we proclaim we can do whatever want. But if we are in Christ, we are called to obedience, not as a way to earn God's acceptance, but as a reflection of God's grace. Furthermore, as God's children we are united to one another and again, called to live for the good of one another, "never to put a stumbling block or hinderance in the way of a brother" (Romans 14:13) and to live by God's commands.	Sometimes we justify our behavior believing it shouldn't matter to anyone else. One area you may encounter this in parenting is modest dress. Our culture encourages girls and women to wear whatever makes them feel good ("hot"). But as a believer in Christ, it is not honoring to God to dress in overly revealing clothing. Help your children evaluate right from wrong based on God's Word, not on their limited understanding of what may or may not harm others.
You can do whatever you put your mind to. You have the power within you. Just do it.	We don't like to think of ourselves as weak and needy. Instead, we like to see ourselves as strong. One of the most misapplied Bible verses is Philippians 4:13, "I can do all things through him who strengthens me." This verse is about contentment: We can be content in all circumstances through Christ. We quote it though (often in sporting events) in a way that conjures up the perception that if we have enough faith in Christ, we can do ANYTHING. When we fail to attain what we wanted we tend to think we didn't have enough faith, will-power, or the right mindset. But the Bible tells us that, in and of ourselves, we can do nothing (John 15:5). With this understanding we begin to see everything as God's grace. Furthermore, 2 Corinthians 12:10 states that only when we are weak do we become strong. In other words, we are called to live depending on Jesus, not ourselves.	What if instead of falsely hyping our children up as capable of anything, we started teaching our children they can do nothing? Would this not help them more quickly turn to God in prayer for all things and learn to live dependently on him? As it is, when they are told to "just do it," that they have the power within, and then they fail, the tendency is to beat themselves up and question their worth. How much greater if we encourage them to see we are weak, but God is strong. He is all-powerful and our ever-present help (Psalm 46:1).

The World's Advice	A Gospel Lens	Applying the Gospel to Everyday Encounters
Fake it until you make it.	I once heard a woman at a Christian conference give this as marriage advice. I was flabbergasted. Not only is this contrary to the vulnerability and authenticity touted even by secular psychology, but it encourages Pharisee-like behavior: to look good on the outside even though our hearts may be far from that on the inside. By wearing a "fake" mask we try to live again, as if we are strong, as if we don't need a Savior. Instead of humbly confessing our need or honestly confessing our sin to God and others, we live pridefully as if we have it all together and don't need to rely on the Lord's help. 2 Corinthians 12:10; Isaiah 40:28–31	Sometimes a parent may encourage a child "to fake it, until you make it" when entering an unfamiliar territory where they don't feel like they belong or aren't equipped. For instance, in a new school setting or a job. One might say something along the lines of act like you belong or act like you know what you're doing and before long you will. In doing so we purport a false confidence rather than encouraging our children to be vulnerable, to confess need, or ask for help. Instead let's move them to find their confidence in the Lord (Proverbs 3:26).
Love is love.	The Bible tells us love is from God (1 John 4:7); he is the originator of it and gives us a picture of what love is in the way the Trinity revolves around each member. The cultural narrative is that anyone is free to love romantically whoever they choose because *love is love*. In other words, it matters not who the love is between, love is the same no matter what. But that is not what God, the originator of love, says. God specifies that the marriage relationship (or romantic love) is limited to one man and one woman (Genesis 2:24).	Our children are not only bombarded with *love is love* messaging, but are led to believe that to think otherwise is judgmental and unloving. This topic can't possibly be done justice in this small space, but included in appendix B on page 155 are a few resources specific to sex and also gender because they are ones you will bump up against sooner than you think, making it imperative that you proactively prepare to talk about this with your children.

The World's Advice	A Gospel Lens	Applying the Gospel to Everyday Encounters
Gender fluidity—I am how I feel.	God created male and female in his image. As much as we try to tamper with God's design or assert truth based on our daily feelings, we cannot change who God created us to be. He formed us in our mother's womb, wonderfully and perfectly, as he intended. Anything other is evidence of the fall and contradicts creation. Genesis 1:27, 31; Psalm 139:13–14	Like *love is love*, your children will also encounter gender fluidity. From my experience as a counselor, when children hit puberty the question of "Who am I?" alongside insecurity and peer influence lead many young teens to explore nonbinary gender identification. Therefore, to stay on top of what your child may be wondering about or hearing at school, it's important to have conversation from as early an age as possible about God's good design of males and females. Again, I have included resources in appendix B.
Men and women are the same.	God not only created male and female in his image, but equal in worth and uniquely different. When we try to say both genders are the same or we condemn certain aspects of either sex, we deny God's good creation. But in our distinct differences and God-given roles we come together for the mutual edification of one another. Genesis 1:27; Ephesians 5:22–33; 1 Peter 3:7	When children are just toddlers, they begin noticing the physical differences in girls and boys as well as gender role behavioral differences. While men and women may hold the same jobs and enjoy the same activities, God created us with distinct biological differences and traits. We want our children to feel no shame in who God uniquely made them to be, but to flourish. We also want our children to appreciate differences in the opposite sex. Therefore, talking about the wonderful ways God made male and female different from as a young an age as possible will help both boys and girls.
Sex is nothing.	In today's over-sexualized, hookup culture, sex is thought of as meaningless. For many young people, having sex feeds right into doing whatever makes you happy in the moment. But sex is not nothing. Sex in the context of marriage is a glorious, God-given gift. Song of Solomon; Matthew 19:4–5; 1 Corinthians 6:16; Hebrews 13:4	Like the other narratives about sex and gender, conversations about God's good intent for sex are not something to shy away from. Our children need to know why sex is worth protecting. With younger children, reference the Birds & Bees resource in appendix B. With older children and teens, a great way to engage in this topic is using what you see in movies and TV series as a springboard for discussion. Resources appropriate for this age are also included in the back.

The World's Advice	A Gospel Lens	Applying the Gospel to Everyday Encounters
Teens will be teens.	While we do not have complete control over our teens (or any age child), by no means should we throw our hands up in the air and declare our job as parents pointless when it comes to teens. Our teens need us to be the authority, set boundaries, and not hand them over to live however they want. Deuteronomy 6:7; Deuteronomy 11:19; Proverbs 22:6; 1 Timothy 3:4; Proverbs 19:18; Proverbs 29:17	As your children become teens, you will likely hear other parents shake their heads and say, "What can you do? Teens will be teens." Teens will be teens if you abdicate your authority. But like the farmer patiently sowing, keep tending the soil. Now is not the time to let it go. You may be worn out, but the harvest has not yet come.
Other Christians are doing _____, so it must be fine. My child will be left out if he/she doesn't have _____.	We justify certain behaviors or sin because other Christians are engaging in these behaviors (or worse). The behaviors may have even become culturally acceptable. But it is idolatry that often leads us to justify certain behavior as acceptable. Proverbs 14:12; Romans 6:1–2	One example of this might be giving our child a phone or access to certain apps because everyone else is. Our idol of acceptance and our not wanting our child to feel left out may blind us to God's wisdom and prevent us from enforcing or setting restrictions.

God's Upside-Down Kingdom

Looking through the lens of God's Word we see that God's wisdom turns the world's wisdom upside down. It also turns our parenting upside down from what the world around us tells us. Everything about God's kingdom—what he says is valuable—is not what the world values. Momentary pleasure, fame, success, material goods, instant gratification, self-glory, the things we look to as the be-all and end-all are fleeting and in direct opposition to the way of Jesus. Nowhere do we see more of the upside-down living of Jesus than in Paul's letter to the Philippians:

> Do nothing from selfish ambition or conceit, but in humility count others more significant than yourselves. Let each of you look not only to his own interests, but

also to the interests of others. Have this mind among yourselves, which is yours in Christ Jesus, who, though he was in the form of God, did not count equality with God a thing to be grasped, but emptied himself, by taking the form of a servant, being born in the likeness of men. And being found in human form, he humbled himself by becoming obedient to the point of death, even death on a cross. Therefore God has highly exalted him and bestowed on him the name that is above every name, so that at the name of Jesus every knee should bow, in heaven and on earth and under the earth, and every tongue confess that Jesus Christ is Lord, to the glory of God the Father. (Philippians 2:3–11)

Jesus counted his equality with God as something not to be grasped. He left the non-stop worship in heaven to take on the form of a servant. Jesus, who is worthy of all glory, left it behind to stoop beneath us, taking on all our sin so that we could be brought into relationship with God.

The very character and nature of God has always been to serve others. To pour out self, to fill others up. To deny self. To die to self for selfish, self-centered people like us. Without the Spirit at work in us, we aren't like him at all. Naturally everything in us wants to grab for self-glory, so we naturally gravitate to what we think the world offers. The ugly way this affects our parenting is that we often make our children into part of our attempt to find self-glory. We want to take pride in them and their accomplishments. We want their behavior and lives to show the world that we are great parents. The result for us is dissatisfaction—we can never be satisfied with something we weren't made for. And the result for our kids is that they feel pressured. Instead of going down the well-worn path of the world, let's follow the gospel of Christ. For the gospel is not simply the way to salvation, it is a way of life—a way of laying down our lives for others. We must commit ourselves to the way of daily repentance and faith because we need to constantly be reoriented to the truth.

What Are We Feasting On?

You've heard the saying, "You are what you eat." Our health is generally linked to our diet. If we fill up on sugar or fatty foods our bodies won't function as designed, but with balanced portions of protein, fruits, vegetables, healthy carbs, vitamins and water, our bodies and minds have the energy we need. In the same way, who we are is reflected in how we spend our time, what we listen to, talk about, where we focus our thoughts, how we invest our resources. "For where your treasure is, there your heart will be also" (Matthew 6:21).

But for us as parents, whatever our treasure is will likely be where our children also seek treasure. Or to put it this way, our idols often become theirs. Therefore, what we feed on matters not just for us, but our children. Without constantly hearing the gospel, being in God's Word, and connecting with the church body, our affection wanes. Therefore, we must be diligent not to neglect the means God has invited us to use to draw near to him.

Knowing our influence on our kids can feel weighty, but hopefully it will also motivate us to consider what we are feasting on. Additionally, I hope we see the direct correlation between being Word-saturated and our ability to decipher truth. The more disconnected we are from God's Word the more easily we are blown by the wind of false doctrine and worldly thought (Ephesians 4:14). Consequently, when we buy into the platitudes, philosophies, and practices such as the ones we've examined, we will compound for our children what they already absorb from the world. What they need desperately is a counter voice to the cultural tide of popular opinion coming at them.

Contrary to what we might think, research points to parents as the primary influence on children even throughout the teen years when it comes to spirituality.[2] In fact, University of Notre Dame sociologist Christian Smith reports that nothing else, not even youth group or Christian school, even come "remotely close to matching the influence of parents on the religious faith and practice of youth."[3] What we do matters. How we see and talk about things will shape our kids.[4]

I want to leave you with a couple scenarios, so you get a bit more of a practical feel for how wearing your gospel glasses directs conversations with your children in a way that helps them see the gospel in everyday life.

Scene 1

Isabella is sitting with friends in the middle school cafeteria. The group begins discussing weekend plans, but Isabella knows one of the girls at the table wasn't included in the group text. Isabella isn't the one who initiated the plans, but she has on gospel glasses, what should she do?

It would be easy to justify that since she is not the one in charge it is out of her hands and there is nothing she can do. Many of the girls at the table may not even think beyond themselves to consider how excluded and alone the girl must feel. I see this occur frequently, not just with adolescents but adults who care only that they were invited. Or who are unwilling to stick their neck out to stand up for someone else. But with gospel glasses, Isabella notices and acts to include the left-out girl, even at the risk of other girls being upset with her. That is what loving our neighbor as ourselves looks like. Living from a place of having received grace, we seek to extend compassion and grace on others.

Scene 2

Mason is at the birthday slumber party of one of his baseball friends when one of the boys pulls out his phone and tells the others he has something to show them. The boys gather around and, though Mason is in the back, he sees enough to know it is a pornographic website. All the other boys want to see more, but Mason has on gospel glasses, what should he do?

Because of ongoing conversations with his parents about the dangers of pornography, Mason knows how pornographic images lead to impure thoughts, desires, and behaviors. He also knows it's important to tell his parents that he was exposed to it. And because he cares about his friends, he doesn't want them to go down this sinful destructive path. While he could directly ask the boys to not continue looking at the pictures, he chooses a different tactic—distraction.

"Hey guys, I'm going to play basketball outside, who wants to come with me?"

Whether the other boys follow or not, Mason is wise to remove himself from the temptation, and offer an alternative for the others. Ultimately, he can't control what each of them do. But the next morning when his parents pick him up, he knows he must tell them what happened so they can handle the situation from there.

Whether role-playing with our kids or using real-life situations, opportunities abound for conversations that get to the heart of what following Jesus looks, sounds, and acts like in our world. In doing so, you increase their awareness of self and others, give them the tools to think and act, and show them practically how looking through the lens of the gospel impacts how we live. For all of this, it should be an everyday prayer that we would keep our gospel glasses on to help us see clearly and that we would teach our kids the unfolding story of the Bible, so they too learn how to filter all things through the lens of the gospel. And when you notice that you have taken them off, you can say sorry to God and to your children, which will help them see that turning to God in repentance is always the way to put your gospel glasses back on.

Questions for Reflection and Discussion:

1. How does seeing the Bible as one unfolding story of God as opposed to an instruction book change how we view particular Bible verses or stories?
2. Are there other platitudes or philosophies that you need to run through the autorefractor gospel lens?
3. What ideas do you have about how best to shepherd your child in an upside-down world?
4. What issues feel most pressing now and how might you initiate or role-play those with your children?

Chapter 6
Stop Hurrying the Hurt

Faith develops out of the most difficult aspects
of our existence, not the easiest.
— EUGENE PETERSON

STARTING WHEN OUR kids are just in diapers, we try to distract tears and negative emotions with a treat. At the pediatrician's office, we are ready with a lollipop after kids get a shot. As a "cure" after a long day at school, we go for ice cream. We hand them iPads or turn on the television in the SUV to appease them while accompanying us on boring errands. We have to keep them happy, it seems, at all costs.

It is no different as our children get older, only maybe more costly (in more ways than one)! With girls especially, we may engage in a little retail therapy, as if a new outfit can make things better. We spend money on a dinner, concert, or a getaway weekend that exceeds our means in an effort to lessen their sadness. Sometimes we give in to plans that we aren't comfortable with, rationalizing that if it snaps them out of their funk it is worth it—just this once. While these indulgences aren't always wrong, I want us to think deeper about how and why we can be so quick to smooth over the hard.

Many of us don't know what to do with emotions like sadness, grief, loss, or disappointment. We aren't comfortable with these "negative" emotions for ourselves and sure don't know how to sit in them with others. Our kids pick up on this. In fact, many of my adolescent clients tell me that when they try to talk to their parents about negative feeling or struggles, they feel shut down. Instead of parents accepting the open invitation into their kids' hearts and minds (the very thing parents of teens long for and complain about not getting) we miss opportunities, shrugging them off with pat responses:

- You shouldn't feel that way.
- It will all work out.
- Suck it up, you don't have anything to be sad about.
- You are so sensitive (or dramatic).
- God doesn't want you to be sad.
- Look on the positive side...
- God's got this.

Talk about platitudes. Aside from not filtering these pithy phrases through a gospel lens, when we say things like these, we make ourselves unsafe. By these responses, our kids learn not to come to us with hard things because of how we minimize and dismiss their feelings and concerns. Furthermore, in trying to hurry the hurt away, we inadvertently communicate something is wrong with them simply for feeling the way they do.

Why can't we just let hard be hard?

Likely, our idols are at play. We don't want our kids to experience any adversity, so instead of looking through our gospel glasses to see how we can speak into a difficult or painful situation, we do whatever we can to minimize and avert. But when we habitually brush over negative emotions and try to shield our kids from all things hard, as they get older and encounter setback or suffering of any kind, they won't be equipped to endure. Instead, they will fall apart, feel like an unjust victim, or fear that God is mad at them. What a difference it can make in our children's lives, though, when we prepare them with a theology of suffering.

Learn God's Theology of Suffering

Just the word *theology* can sound intimidating. But a theology of suffering is simply what God says about suffering, its purposes, and our response to it. Just as we need to know from God why we can cling to hope, understanding how a good God allows for suffering helps us endure *with hope*. To this end, let's look at how a biblical theology of suffering can reshape our circumstances and how it can also reshape our parenting.

1. Suffering is universal.

> Beloved, do not be surprised at the fiery trial when it comes upon you to test you, as though something strange were happening to you. (1 Peter 4:12)

> "In the world you will have tribulation." (John 16:33)

Whether in the form of everyday frustrations or unsurmountable grief, we all experience suffering of various degrees throughout our lives. Some trials are a consequence of our sin or someone else's. Other times suffering comes for no other reason than we live in a broken world. Remember Act 2 of God's story: because of the fall, everything in this world is tainted by sin and destruction. Even the fact that our clothes wear out and our cars break down points to the reality that God's good design of all creation has been turned on its head. Therefore, instead of being shocked by sin and suffering, the real surprise is when things actually are as originally intended to be. When Moses pointed out to the Israelites that after forty years in the wilderness their clothing didn't wear out, he was making the point that in a broken world *this* was not normal (Deuteronomy 8:4). Apart from God's grace, the world and everything in it is breaking and falling apart.

When we see the universality of suffering, it shifts our perspective from what we sometimes presume about suffering—that we are the only one experiencing hardship or that God uses trials like "karma," to pay people back for the bad things they do. No, God doesn't work that way. Quite the contrary, as sinners with hearts naturally set against God, we don't deserve any good thing, and yet God pours out his grace, protection, and love all the time. God uses even suffering for his good purposes, which makes the Christian view of suffering unique.

2. Suffering unites us with Christ.

> For as we share abundantly in Christ's sufferings, so through Christ we share abundantly in comfort too. (2 Corinthians 1:5)

> that I may know Him and the power of His resurrection and the fellowship of His sufferings, being conformed to His death. (Philippians 3:10 NASB)

Jesus left the glory and perfection of heaven to enter a messed-up, broken world—willingly! Though a King, nothing about his life on this earth was glamorous. Scripture tells us that even his physical appearance was unappealing (Isaiah 53:2). Jesus was poor, from a small town in a small corner of the world. He was King of the universe, but he never demanded respect or special treatment. He had nothing to prove. Not once did he insist on validation or being understood, and never did he allow his feelings to sinfully rule. Rather, he endured the mistreatment, false accusations, slander, rejection, abuse, even death by the people he came to save. How unlike him we are, but how very much he knows what it is like for us in our suffering.

He came to make a way to redeem sinners to the Father, but to also identify with us. Because he came in the flesh and lived among us as one of us, he understands all that we go through. There is nothing we experience that he didn't also experience. Therefore, we can go to him, and he "gets" us even when maybe nobody else does.

But being united to him in suffering also means that we "get" more of who he is as the Man of Sorrows. His life on earth was full of suffering, and yet he perfectly and sinlessly endured until death. In doing so, he ensured our suffering would end. Remember Acts 3 and 4 of God's story—all things will be redeemed. He will make all things new. He has already conquered sin to ensure that those who know him will spend all eternity with him. Therefore, we look to him for the hope of heaven, where there will be no more tears. We look to him to help us endure, knowing we are not alone.

3. Suffering changes and grows us.

We rejoice in our sufferings, knowing that suffering produces endurance, and endurance produces character, and character produces hope. (Romans 5:3–4)

Count it all joy, my brothers, when you meet trials of various kinds, for you know that the testing of your faith produces steadfastness. And let steadfastness have its full effect, that you may be perfect and complete, lacking in nothing. (James 1:2–4)

Before I was afflicted I went astray, but now I keep your word. (Psalm 119:67)

No one wants to invite suffering into their lives. Naturally we go out of our way to keep suffering at bay, especially as parents. But how many times have you heard, and maybe even said this yourself, that though you wouldn't wish certain suffering on anyone, what the suffering led to, they (or you) would not undo? This is because of exactly what these verses reveal—suffering has a way of growing us into maturity and moving us into a deeper relationship with God. As we notice this, we discover what it means to rejoice in suffering.

I am thankful for the suffering God has allowed in my life and the lives of my husband and children. With my daughter's permission, I have shared that as a teen she struggled with an eating disorder and depression. Walking alongside her in that long season was a lonely, difficult time. There is much I could say about our experiences in the trenches that still stirs up lots of emotion, but in looking back, I see how God used hard things for our good. Both my daughter and I learned more of what it looks like to live in dependence on Jesus. I came to embrace my weakness and need in a way I never had before. I grew in empathy and grace for others. I became less judgmental. I've seen the way God has used my daughter in the lives of so many other girls. And for both of us, this trial set us on a path to becoming helping professionals. Neither one of us was left unchanged, for our good and to the glory of God.

Another aspect of change produced through suffering is growing us in obedience. Through suffering we come to face our own sin, even when the suffering is not because of our sin. For instance, in suffering and trials, my anger revealed my lack of faith and desire to be my own god. My idol of comfort was also challenged. I didn't want the inconvenience or the deviation from my agenda that happens when trials come. Nor did I want to be stretched to deal with conflict, and yet the call to redemptive living moves us to forsake our comfort and forge ahead in seeking forgiveness and restoration.

Without trials, we could remain superficially at peace with others but never have our self-centered thoughts or feelings revealed, including jealousy, judgment, revenge, or entitlement to name just a few. Of course, none of us want to see the ugliness in our hearts, but we can't repent of what we don't see. And the more we are aware of sin and see Christ's compassion moving toward us in our sin, the more we desire to live in a way that glorifies him. Suffering is one way that God uses to grow us in obedience, holiness, and Christ-likeness.

4. Suffering points us heavenward.

But rejoice insofar as you share Christ's sufferings, that you may also rejoice and be glad when his glory is revealed. (1 Peter 4:13)

And after you have suffered a little while, the God of all grace, who has called you to his eternal glory in Christ, will himself restore, confirm, strengthen, and establish you. (1 Peter 5:10)

Suffering reminds us of the bottom line—this world is not our home.

When things are comfortable, when life is great, when we experience no hardships, it is easy to not think about Jesus. We don't need him; everything here and now is satisfying to us. While contentment is great, if we go back to the closed hand/ open palm idolatry litmus test, we may realize that the reason we fall apart when things in this world get knocked off kilter is because we are looking for "life" in the things of this world. But the more the things in this world fail to deliver, the more we long for another world. Hardship, trials, suffering have a way of keeping us looking heavenward.

I don't know about you, but the longer I've lived in the brokenness and sin of this world, the more I yearn for Christ's return, for all things to be made right. Suffering does that, whether my own or witnessing the suffering of others across the globe. The more we are exposed to suffering, the more we want redemption. It creates an ache, an unsettling, that causes us to fix our eyes on the promise. As Christians, we know victory has been won. Satan has been defeated. Darkness will not win the day. Christ will come and all things will be made new. This is our great hope. It helps us endure.

Our children probably don't yet feel the same longing for Jesus's return. When I was younger (even a younger adult), I remember thinking, "Not yet, God, I still have my bucket list." However, when things aren't right, may we always be reminding our kids that this is not our home. As you may have heard it said, we are just traveling through, as sojourners awaiting our permanent home. Without suffering, we don't feel our true status. Suffering reminds us, encourages us even, that we haven't arrived yet at our final destination. So, when things aren't as they should be, as my husband likes to say, "We can endure the suck." This here and now is not our forever. Our kids need to be coached in this!

I posed the question at the beginning of the chapter, "What difference might a theology of suffering make?" I hope being reminded that suffering comes not because God is out to get you but because God is working good in you helps to shift your own perspective on suffering. Seeing through gospel glasses, I hope you are also now able to hand those glasses to your kids to help them see more clearly what God is up to in our suffering.

The difference a robust theology of suffering will make is a more rooted hope in him in all things, and the ability to persevere. It doesn't mean there won't still be sadness, grief, doubts, and questions. But we know from the Psalms that God is big enough to handle our every emotion and welcomes us to come to him with it all. But as we also see from the psalmists, even in angst over suffering and while wondering when God will intervene, what still comes through is a resolute, "I will trust you." It is one of those, "I believe; help my unbelief!" (Mark 9:24). And that is my prayer for us all—that he would help us trust him when life doesn't make sense and the hard feels never-ending. That we would be comforted and upheld by his Word about who he is and the "for just a little while" suffering would pale in comparison to an eternity with him.

Questions for Reflection and Discussion

1. What is your biggest takeaway about suffering from this chapter?
2. Have you seen God's goodness in suffering? If so, how? Is this something you can or have shared with your child?
3. In thinking about eternity, how would you fill in the blank of this statement? *One day there will be (or there will not be)* _____. Perhaps, this question could be used with the family to imagine together what will be done away with, and what we will gain for all eternity when Christ returns. Maybe even have each family member draw a picture.
4. Take some time to read through the Psalms, and then use one of them to write out your own prayer. To get you started, some of my go-to psalms in times of trials and suffering include Psalms 13, 16, 23, 24, 27, 34, 40, 46, 55, and 136.

Part III:
A Redemptive Plan

HOPEFULLY AFTER READING Part I and Part II, you are convinced more than ever that long-range, redemptive parenting is the way forward. Even more than that, I hope you are convinced of the redeeming love of Jesus for you and your children. We will never be the perfect parents and our children will never be the perfect children, but we do have a perfect Savior who never tires of showering us with his grace.

While this section will flesh out what parenting redemptively looks like, I want to emphasize again—*there are no parenting formulas that guarantee outcomes.* If there were, it would be on us to be the perfect parents. What a burden that would be! Thankfully, it's not all about us or all up to us. We and our children have a perfect heavenly Father and the gift of relationship with him through Jesus. Seeing our sins and enduring suffering keep us needing Jesus. Working through our sin and suffering with one another in our families and elsewhere in a redemptive manner grows us in dependence on Jesus, in Christ-likeness, and brings glory to the Lord. With that in mind, let's dive in to see what redemptive parenting is all about.

Chapter 7
Redemptive Living

Our honesty about our sins and imperfections
will send a message to our children that they can sin
and find grace and that they can mess up
and have hope, for all people are imperfect.

— BOB KELLEMEN

AS WE BEGIN thinking about what it is to live out the gospel in our homes, let's begin by thinking about the shaping influence of our childhood. For me, some of those shaping influences include my race, birth order (firstborn), and family makeup (having one sister, married parents, and a stay-at-home mom). Added to those influences were living in the same community my entire upbringing, always going to church, and attending public schools. All these things and many others contributed to who I am and how I see things in the world. I didn't have control over any of these influences. We all have shaping influences—good, bad, and neutral—that have nothing to do with us and at the same time everything to do with who we are. Quite often we are unaware of how we are being shaped by different life experiences.

The same, of course, is true for our children. Even what is outside of *our* control will shape them. That does not mean our kids are doomed by any negative shaping influences. Nor does what is outside our control render us helpless. Far from it. We have an incredible opportunity as parents to shape how our children interpret life. What we say and do, how we speak into and handle various circumstances will serve to shape them. As will silence or inaction.

My friend Megan Michelson of Birds & Bees says that if you don't teach your kids about sex, your silence teaches them that it's not okay to talk about it with you.[1] In other words, abdication in our role as parents will shape our kids in the same way speaking or not speaking into a topic does. Therefore, we need to proactively consider the long-term effects of our shaping influence on our children—both what we want our shaping influence to be about and what we hope for it not to be.

We've already established that, as sinful humans, we will not do everything right. At times our words and actions will hurt our children. But the beautiful thing about living redemptively in our homes is that dealing honestly and openly about our sin actually becomes a positive shaping influence. Did you get that? How incredible is it that when we deal honestly with what we do wrong, it will positively shape our children! Of course, the reverse is true too; when we sweep sin under the rug and don't deal with honestly, that too is a shaping influence on our children.

But let's back up a bit to see what redemptive living even entails!

What Is Redemptive Living?

Redemption is a slave market term used for the purchase price paid to set a slave free. It means to purchase out of bondage. It's the buyback price, which includes acting to save someone from error or evil. Consider then Jesus our Redeemer. His perfect life and substitutionary death were the redemption price necessary to release us from sin's slavery and into a life with him. He bought us out of bondage.

Taking the concept of redemption into the context of our homes and relationships, to live redemptively is to live compelled by grace and mercy. It means owning up to our sin. Instead of hiding sin, dismissing sin, or justifying sin, we honestly confess our sin to one another. It also means accepting one's confession and extending forgiveness instead of holding sin over one another.

When we give grace and mercy to one another we reflect the heart of Jesus by not demanding others pay for their sins. Rather we set them free from sin's penalty and absorb the cost ourselves. So, living redemptively is living out the reality of the gospel with one another as we confess, repent, forgive, give grace, and restore one another. All of which should form a normal pattern in our homes, each one flowing out of the other.

As the parents, we must go first. Our children will learn it is safe to confess not because they are told the Bible tells us to but when they see *us* model humble confession. Your willingness to admit sin and, when you've been hurt, give forgiveness and grace shows them they can too. Either way your children will learn from you how to handle their sin, struggles, and failures.

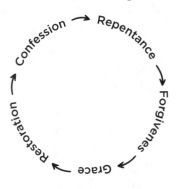

The pattern of confession, repentance, forgiveness, grace, and restoration provides a true picture of who God is. God welcomes sinners to come boldly to him. He doesn't require penance or keep a record of wrongs. But this isn't a reality many Christians live in. Instinctively we think we must clean ourselves up before we can go to God or show back up at church. We think God is mad at us. Maybe this is the message—a shaping influence—you got as a kid.

Recently a mom sitting behind me at a football game said to her young misbehaving son that "God is so, so, so mad at you right now." Everything in me wanted to turn around, scoop him up, and tell him, "No he is not! That's not who God is!" Sadly, this false message about who God is will likely follow him into adulthood. He will either do his darnedest to perfectly follow all the rules in order to keep God happy, or he'll run as far from God as he can because who wants to feel like they are living under God's frown?

Redemptive Living in the Nitty Gritty of Parenting

Sometimes our sin may be blatantly obvious, but not always. So if we are to go first in confessing sin, you may wonder how we can be more alert to our sin. First, growing in awareness of our sin is part of growing in grace and Christ-likeness. As we become more attuned to what's going on in our hearts by recognizing ruling idols and wrong motives, the more readily we will identify sin. But identifying those sinful idols and motivations often comes only when we humbly go before God in prayer asking him to search out our heart to help us see the ways we go wrong without even noticing (Psalm 139:23–24).

The problem with noticing sin in ourselves is that we all have a vested interest in staying blind to our sins (yet being really good at noticing others'). But, if you recall from chapter 4, our emotions can give us a clue. Take for example, anger. Say you lose it on your kids after listening to them bicker off and on all day. It would be easy to rationalize your yelling. After all, you were patient long enough and if they would have been more loving, you wouldn't have had to respond as you did. But the truth is, their misbehavior does not justify your sin. You disciplined out of anger, not because they made you, but because you have sin within you. And, at the moment you went off on them, it is likely the idol of comfort was ruling your heart. Not a wrong desire, but could it be that your failure to address the bickering earlier and your eventual explosion point to ruling desires that are greater than a love for God and shepherding your children?

Seeing and admitting sin is not easy. But we will never escape the reality of sin in our lives. And it is in the nitty gritty of it where you have the opportunity to live out the gospel with your kids and in other relationships. Whether anger, judgment, gossip, or something else, when you come to see these things as sin, doing the vulnerable, hard thing of repentance and confession is how we live redemptively with one another and help our children learn to do the same. I will admit this is easier said than done. On my own I wouldn't be able to; it is only through the prompting of the Spirit and strength of the Lord that comes through prayer.

Everyone is different, so what you say will be different, but here is what modeling redemptive living might look like for you as the parent:

> "Please forgive me for disciplining you out of anger. I was worried about what other people would think of me which led to me to act out in anger toward you. Would you pray for me that I would not let the fear of man drive my actions?"

You may wonder about using "fear of man" with a young child (more on this in the next chapter), but as a parent I want you to take notice of three things this short script helps accomplish.

1. The parent modeling confession and repentance to a child helps the child feel safer to share his/her own sin.
2. The parent specifically identifying the ruling idol helps the child become aware of and start to pay attention to the root sin (fear of man) beneath the surface sin (anger).

3. The parent talking about his/her root sin opens the door to further spiritual conversation.

Even if your children are young and don't "get" all this, they are being shaped by what you say and do. Likewise, they are shaped by our response when called out for sin. Sometimes in our sin we're blind and unaware of what's going on in our hearts, so we don't know we need to repent. Just consider when you've been bitter toward someone for something they know nothing about. In those cases, we need to go to that person instead of harboring anger. It's not easy, but this too is what living redemptively is.

Before we discuss approaching others when they have sinned against us, let me first offer one caveat: sometimes we don't need to go to them. We don't need to keep a record of every offense (Proverbs 19:11). Rather, we need to cover it with grace. When we absorb being sinned against, this too is redemptive living. So before going to someone about their sin, I would caution you to check your own heart. The Bible says, "first take the log out of your own eye, and then you will see clearly to take the speck out of your brother's eye" (Matthew 7:5). Along with inspecting for your own sin, evaluate if or why it is important to deal with. Sometimes it is.

My adult daughter is leading the way for me in this area. There have been many times I've been oblivious to something I said, did, or didn't do that deeply hurt her. How grateful I am that she has come to me, instead of stuffing it and growing resentful toward me. To think how our relationship could have so easily become ruptured had she not done the hard thing of letting me know how I hurt her. It can be hard to hear, but not nearly as hard as the alternative. In fact, when I've said or done something to hurt someone and have no idea until much later it feels so much worse. Had I only known, I could have sought forgiveness so much sooner.

Furthermore, when someone distances themselves from us and we have no idea why, we start making assumptions based on false narratives and treating people accordingly. Several times after these types of situations have happened with friends, I've thought, *Gosh, how much time of missed friendship and hurt feelings could have been saved if we had just dealt honestly with it, if we had lived redemptively!*

Another repercussion of not dealing honestly with our sin before our kids is that, as they get older, they will stop sharing with us. Think about it: if we habitually sweep our sin under the rug, pretending it's not there, resentment builds up in our children when we call them out on theirs and they see us as hypocrites. Not only that, but we are seen as unsafe for them to share their sin or struggles with when we aren't willing to acknowledge ours.

But it's amazing what *Please forgive me* can do.

"I'm so sorry I did _____. I was being ruled by my own selfish desires and was unwilling to sacrifice what I wanted for you. Will you please forgive me?"

Hearts soften when we are brutally honest, name the sin for what it is, and not just give a blanket, "I'm sorry that hurt you." This, of course, does not mean there may not still be hurt. We will have to talk through feelings and what happened to get to true reconciliation, but a genuine confession is the first step toward giving and getting grace. Even still, we are often unwilling to be exposed, so we cover up and pretend. When we do, our kids learn to do the same. At the same time, walls go up that keep our relationships on a superficial level.

To recap, owning up to our sin is step one in living redemptively in our homes. I keep reiterating this point, but remember we will all sin. That's a given. So the important thing is what we do with our sin! Do we pretend it's not there and sweep it under the rug, or do we deal honestly with it before God and others? When we put our sin on the table as regular repenters, we show our kids by word and deed that we are sinners in need of Jesus. They need to see us in this way. Seeing our need helps them see their own need. Furthermore, when honest confession and repentance is the normal pattern in our homes, we move past law-driven, surface-level conversation, to the heart. This is because regular repenting calls not for just naming external bad behavior but the *why* underneath it. In other words, the desire or motive behind the behavior. To draw upon the earlier example, identifying the root, or idol, in a confession could also sound something like this:

"Mommy snapped, please forgive me. I was unwilling to sacrifice for your good. My selfish desires were ruling me and, at that moment, I only wanted to sit in my chair and drink my coffee with no one needing me."

We don't like to go there, do we? When I think about what keeps us from being regular repenters, pride tops the list. We refuse to humble ourselves or see ourselves as needy of grace. Fear and shame are also wrapped up in our unwillingness to be *that* honest. Perhaps our fear stems from worry that if we let our kids into our sin then we can't get on them about theirs. Or maybe we think we will lose any authority to tell them not to do *xyz* when we do the same.

Satan would love for these fears to keep us from confession and honest conversation. But when we try to hide, we create a facade that keeps our kids from freely coming to us. Then we wonder why they won't open up! I hear this often in the counseling room—parents complaining that their kids won't talk. While I'm not saying the reason always points back to whether or not we are living redemptively, certainly it is a huge factor. The teens I counsel confirm it is true. If Mom or Dad even admitted their sin and apologized, they say things might be different. I agree. When we're honest, and our kids hear us confess our idols and ask for forgiveness, a beautiful thing happens, they feel free to do the same.

When our kids see we are in the same boat, they will be less afraid to confess and deal honestly with their sin. We make it safe for them to be regular repenters. And when our kids share with us their sin, and we identify with them instead of doling out condemnation or making them feel shame, they'll be more apt to keep coming to us as a safe person.

Here are a couple examples to showcase the difference between identifying with them or not.

When one of my sons was caught doing something wrong, we learned that the reason he did stemmed from a desire to look good in front of his friends. Well, I absolutely get that! I too say and do things at times to look good in the eyes of others—remember *fear of man*! So while my son still experienced consequences for his behavior, my husband and I were able to identify with him in his sin and come alongside him with compassion. He in turn felt safe to talk to us not just after that incident, but going forward.

A counter example is a story one of our children shared with me about a friend who had been hiding sin from her parents. After she was caught, her mom shared something she had done in the past that the daughter had not previously known. Because the daughter had only seen her mom in a perfect light, she had not felt safe to be honest with her mom about her sin and struggles. Instead, she had lived hiding in shame.

While using discretion is wise when it comes to what we divulge to our kids about our past and present sin, if we present ourselves as anything other than fellow fallen sinners, it's not likely our kids will feel safe to confide in us. But I have found in counseling teens that, rather than them feeling like they have the green light to do certain things that they learned their parent did as a teenager, hearing their parents' stories helped them better understand why they shouldn't. At the same time, they feel more comfortable talking about things they might otherwise hide from their parents.

Sometimes we can project an aura of perfection without realizing it. This was the case for me with my daughter. One day when she was in college, she called me stressed out and upset. As I was in mid-sentence with my response, she interrupted and asked to talk to Dad instead. *What in the world! She called my cell phone to talk to ME!* Nevertheless, I handed *my* phone to my husband.

When he hung up with her, he gently conveyed to me that the reason she requested him is because I wasn't being relatable. He went on to say that she needed me to identify with her, not try to fix her. What my "fix it" mode conveyed to my daughter were all the ways she wasn't measuring up to my perfection. In other words, she didn't see me in the same boat as a struggling sinner. She saw me as having it all together without any struggles.

That is certainly not true, but my lack of vulnerability paired with my high self-sufficiency witnessed to my own strength, not someone living desperately dependent on Jesus. The sad result? For my daughter I had become unsafe to confide in.

A beautiful thing happened, though, when I begin to speak more honestly about my sin: I became more human to her. Instead of my daughter viewing me badly because of my sin, she drew closer to me. She was able then to have conversations with me that she had reserved for my husband. She had needed me to go first, to let down my guard, to show her I wasn't perfect, and she didn't need to try to be perfect either.

The best part of our children seeing us as imperfect is the OPPORTUNITY to tell our children again and again about why we need Jesus, and how he is everything that we are not. This is the good news of the gospel that is often left off— Christ's perfection for us. He lived the perfect life for us and it is his perfect record that God sees when he looks upon those who are his.

To think, as Tim Keller has often said, "We are more sinful and flawed in ourselves than we ever dared believe, yet at the very same time we are more loved and accepted in Jesus Christ than we ever dared hope." This understanding of our standing before God is vital; without it we will not go boldly to his throne of grace, and the effects of staying hidden will keep a barrier up in our relationships. When we "get" the truth—that God is not mad at us, that he is not condemning us according to our sin or disqualifying us from his love, but instead smiling at us because of Jesus's perfection, we become free.

Free to admit our sin.

Free from beating ourselves up over our failures.

Free to be loved.

Free to live under grace and give grace to others.

One summer my daughter was home for a month during college. I had a manuscript due in September, so I was counting on making great headway in the writing process during the month of July and that is exactly what I prioritized. Well, my preoccupation with writing made my daughter feel less important, as if I cared more about my book than spending time with her. She called me out on this. (This was after our previous episode with her not feeling safe to share honestly with me!)

Through a hard conversation, I came to see my schedule and time as a ruling idol. Anything that interferes with my plans makes me anxious that what I need to do isn't going to get done. Because of my idol, I made her feel less than. I needed to repent of my ruling idol, trust God with my time, and reorient my priorities so she knew she was more important.

That next morning, I ditched my workout class (another part of my schedule I'm not very flexible about) and made the choice to spend time with my daughter. I decided to trust that God would give me the time I needed to stay on track with my writing. My daughter needed to hear from me that she was more valuable. But she also needed to *see* by my actions that she was more valuable. I had to confess my sin and ask her for forgiveness.

From living redemptively in our home, some things I've noticed and am thankful for:

- My kids have compassion toward others in their sin.
- They are quick to forgive and give grace.
- They are aware of their heart motives.
- They see their need for Jesus.
- They talk to us openly.
- No topic is off limits.

I also have great hope that living redemptively will impact their marriages and other relationships. I've already seen this with our daughter's interaction with her roommates when she was in college and now with her husband. But living redemptively doesn't just happen. From young ages, our kids watch and learn from us by how we relate to them, our spouses, and others.

If we are not confessing our sin, we can't expect they will feel free to divulge their sin, struggles, or what is really going on in their hearts. As with many other things, our actions speak louder than our words. You've probably heard said, "More is caught than taught." If we teach the importance of confessing sin, but they see us act in a contrary way, they will likely act as we do, not as we say. If this is where you find yourself, grace to you! It's never too late to change course!

Questions for Reflection and Discussion:

1. Why is it so hard to confess sin and live redemptively—not just with our kids, but with our spouses, friends, other family members?

2. What role does prayer play for you in living redemptively? Are there any ways you feel prompted to change your prayer life in order to better embody redemptive living?

3. Do you envision it being hard to take first steps for living redemptively and, if so, why? And how do you think your child will respond?

4. How do you think living redemptively in your household all the time could change the aura of your home?

Chapter 8
Building a Foundation for Engaging the Heart

*When we focus on good behavior, we end up with kids
who worry about impressing God and for whom the good news
is an afterthought. . . . The good news means you relate
to God based on what Jesus has done for you,
not what you've done to prove yourself worthy.*

— JACK KLUMPENHOWER

YEARS AGO, WHILE I was leading a middle school girls Bible study, I realized that, though the girls were in church-going families, very few of them could articulate the gospel. The very basis of our faith was unclear to them. They had never heard of theological terms like *justification* and *sanctification*, and sin as more than outward behavior was not a concept they had been taught. Also worth noting, most of the teenagers did not attend "big church" with their parents, instead they went to a separate youth room.

I was concerned about their biblical illiteracy, which seemed to be compounded by them not attending the worship service and hearing the sermon. It seemed to me that, at least for some, moralism and how-to's had replaced the good news of the gospel. Also, child-centered programs, though good in theory, often further disconnect families and hinder the vitality of inter-generational relationships within the body.

At the same time, parents are looking to the church, youth workers, and other ministries to handle the spiritual teaching and nourishing of their kids. In much the same way we outsource academic tutoring, specialized sports training, and music lessons to the professionals, we do this with faith as well. But remember—parents, not the church or a youth leader are the number one influencer on a kid's spiritual life.[1]

As the primary shepherds of our kids' hearts, it is not enough to drop them off at church and expect they'll come out knowing all things Jesus and loving him all the days of their lives. What we do, what we talk about, and what we prioritize in our homes is crucial to the spiritual development of our kids. It's out of our everyday talk that our kids learn to put on gospel lenses.

Therefore, "You shall teach them [God's Word] diligently to your children, and shall talk of them when you sit in your house, and when you walk by the way, and when you lie down, and when you rise" (Deuteronomy 6:7).

Spiritual conversations should naturally flow out of our everyday encounters. They are not meant just for Sunday school, or at home only during family devotional times. I imagine that one of the reasons theological and spiritual conversations might not be part of our everyday lives with our families is that we feel ill-equipped. But despite any lack of Bible literacy or deficiency in your spiritual understanding, God has called you to be your child's parent. You are the best parent for your child. And as you seek to lead your child, God will lead you. Remember, dependence is the posture he desires from us.

We don't have to have all the answers or pretend to our kids that we do! Instead, when they ask those hard questions, we can go to God together with our kids and learn side by side. Or simply tell your child that you aren't sure, but you will find out and then come back to the conversation. Then do that—ask your pastor, Bible study teacher, small group leader, or knowledgeable friend for help.

While consulting a pastor, mentor, Bible study leader, or turning to other resources is helpful and wise, also be encouraged that as we study Scripture and grow in our gospel understanding our ability to see life through gospel glasses becomes clearer. To this end, if you are not already, I hope you will seek out a gospel-centered church (see related article link in appendix B on page 155), participate in Bible studies or small groups rooted in God's truth, and spend time reading God's Word and gospel-centered books.

By "gospel-centered," I mean that the focus is the centrality of Christ's work and worth for us, his perfection, his righteousness, his grace alone. Gospel teaching is presented through the lens of Christ and the four movements we discussed earlier—creation, fall, redemption, restoration—as opposed to law, self-effort, good advice, or works-based Christianity that is more focused on us than Jesus.

Gospel-centrality is key because, if the teaching our kids receive is anything but the true gospel of grace, they will trust in their own righteousness, not in what Jesus has done. As the apostle Paul writes, any other teaching is no gospel at all: "I am astonished that you are so quickly deserting him who called you in the grace of Christ and are turning to a different gospel—not that there is another one, but there are some who trouble you and want to distort the gospel of Christ" (Galatians 1:6–7).

When teaching focuses more on behaving better than believing, children will know how to act Christianly, but their hearts will be far from Jesus. To cultivate kids who genuinely love Christ, we must lead them to love the person of Jesus. He must be our emphasis—his worth and work for us along with our desperate need for him because of sin. When our kids begin to grasp the depth of sin, met by his matchless grace, how they relate to God changes. When they know Jesus, they will seek out a church and Christian community when they go off to college or out on their own. This is a miracle of new life that only the

Spirit can do in anyone's heart, no matter their age. But the Lord is pleased to use us to remind our children through our words and actions just how much they need Jesus.

As we live before them by faith, they will notice that our Christian life flows from a love for Jesus. Knowing who we are (sinners deserving death), who God is (a merciful, just God, steadfast in his love for sinners), and who we are because of Christ (sinners saved by grace) is what cultivates a love for Jesus.[2]

So let's not shy away from talking about theological concepts even when our kids seem too young. Continuing in Deuteronomy 6, we see that the day will come when our kids will ask more about what we've been sharing with them: "When your son asks you in time to come, 'What is the meaning of the testimonies and statues'" (Deuteronomy 6:20). This doesn't just happen! It happens because we have intentionally worked to shape their hearts and minds about the things of God.

Another reason parents might not talk to their kids about God, or maybe they do for a time but stop short, is because in the moment it feels futile. We think they aren't listening. They act bored, or even resistant. With no evidence of impact, it feels pointless. It can feel like a lot of work for nothing. But in time, after planting seed after seed (remember the farmer!), Scripture offers us the hope that the day will come when they begin to understand.

Recently I was reading back through a journal I kept when my children were young (well, actually, when my first two were young—the third child has no journal!). In it I came across the story of the time my almost three-year-old son and I were sitting at the kitchen table eating lunch. After tearing up his sandwich, he handed me a piece and said, "This is Christ's body broken for you, Mommy!"

At that age he didn't understand what communion meant, but he watched it happen every Sunday. Seeds were being planted. He continued to regularly feed "communion" to our yellow lab. And then one day several years later he came to know and trust in Christ's body broken for him!

From talking about spiritual things and observing what was taking place in our home and at church, our son's heart was sensitive and ready to embrace the love of Jesus for him at an early age. It is exciting when we see this happen. But remember there are no formulas or guaranteed results. Shaping their hearts and minds toward the truth of God requires keeping at the forefront of our minds what our true hope is for our children. It might not always feel like it, but to consistently pour into our children without any visible "results" is the epitome of long-range parenting.

At the same time, I want you to know if you haven't been cultivating a spiritual landscape in their hearts and your home, it is never too late to start. By God's grace, even without early childhood experiences, teenagers, young adults, middle-aged and older adults come to know the Lord. If you want to make a parenting pivot in this area, consider starting with an honest conversation with your kids, much like what we talked about in the last chapter.

> "William, Sadie, we need to ask for your forgiveness for we have not been diligent in teaching you about Jesus. I know that might sound strange, but more than anything we want you to know him as your Savior so starting fresh, we want to make some changes . . ."

Creating Categories for Understanding the Heart

Perhaps you are overwhelmed at the thought of trying to make big theological concepts and conversations bite-size. In our house, we've done so by creating categories and building upon them. Think of categories, which I'll explain, as foundation-laying.

Without naming it a "category," I've already introduced the category of sin as idolatry. We called our hearts "idol factories," remember? Another one of Paul Tripp's phrases and another category is seeing ourselves as "glory thieves."[3] Think about this term. What does a glory thief do but seek to steal another's glory, praise, and worship, right? This is what we do to God. We try to insert ourselves as king: "Look at me!" "Praise me!" "Serve me!" We want to be worshipped, and at the same time we worship what we think will give us life, so we are glory thieves and idol worshippers at the same time!

By introducing and building upon categories, such as "sin as idolatry," we help our children see themselves rightly and connect their behavior to their hearts. Now I know some of us struggle to think of our precious babies as sinners. We would rather take the world's view that sees kids as inherently good. But this is not what the Bible teaches. The Bible says, "None is righteous, no, not one; no one understands; no one seeks for God. All have turned aside; together they have become worthless; no one does good, not even one" (Romans 3:10–12).

For our kids to know their need for Jesus, they must know they are sinners. So we talk to them about the fall and remind them that, since Adam and Eve, our spiritual DNA is to go our own way. That's how the Bible defines sin (Isaiah 53:6). Why is this so important? People don't come to Jesus who don't know they need him. And unlike what progressive Christianity may say, telling our kids they are sinners will not hurt their self-worth! I would argue that knowing our true condition alongside God's compassion enhances our worth. Despite our sin, we are so valuable to God that he sent his Son to die!

Additionally, when *we* (Mom and Dad) understand our natural bent toward sin, instead of being shocked by our kids' sin, we can respond to theirs with compassion. Our compassion makes it easier for our kids to come to us. And isn't that what we want—children and teens who talk freely with us? On the flip side, when we respond along the lines of, "I can't believe you did that," they feel more shame and will likely be driven to more secrecy and hiding of sin from you. Not only from you, but from your response, they will assume that this is how God treats us in our sin too, which could not be further from the truth. God says, "No matter what you've done, come to me. I love you."

Sin as Idolatry

As a review, the core of all sin is misplaced worship for something other than God. It is the turning away from God to a false god for identity, worth, life. We all do this because we were made for worship. If we aren't worshipping God, we are worshipping something else in his place. That's why the first commandment is, "You shall have no other gods besides me" (Exodus 20:3). When we break any of the other commandments, we automatically break this first one too. For if I steal, covet, or bear false witness against another, I am being ruled by something other than God. Perhaps it's my desire to look better at the expense of someone else. Or, maybe I'm looking to possessions to give me status and acceptance. It's the why behind my actions, which always points to an idol.

Thinking of sin as an idol helps us see more clearly just how broken we are, which exposes our need. So let's also help our children learn to trace their behavior backward. By using the biblical category of idolatry to explain the sin beneath the sin, you give them the glasses to see what's going on beneath the surface, so they can begin detecting their false gods. This helps them see where they are not believing that Jesus is enough.

But we need to remember that, just because our kids can identify their idols, awareness alone will not prevent them from chasing false gods and buying into Satan's lies; just as it doesn't for us. But with the foundational knowledge of who we are and who God is, our hope and prayer is that when sin is exposed, they will go freely to God's throne of grace. If they know Jesus is safe to go to, always forgiving and forever faithful even when they are not, the realities of his love will more likely stir within them a desire to live in a way that is honoring to him (1 John 1:7–10).

Sin as Two Types

By the time they are teenagers, many kids from Christian homes have mastered the art of appearing godly. They have learned to play the Christian game of saying and doing the "right" things when others are watching. For example, they might regularly attend youth group, even lead worship, go to Christian summer camp, and post Bible verses on their social media, but their hearts could still be far from God. Hidden beneath their performance or goodness may be outright rebellion. These are the kids doing all the Christian things but drinking, getting high, and/or having sex when out of the public eye. Others might be so filled with self-righteous pride because of their "good" behavior that they live as if they don't really need a Savior.

Tim Keller in his book *The Prodigal God*, unpacks the story of the two brothers from Luke 15 to help us see how sin can fall into one of two types—elder-brother sin or younger-brother sin.[4] Younger-brother sin is what we tend to think of when we think of sin. It is the external bad behavior. Whereas elder-brother sin is the hidden pride and self-righteous, judgmental motivations in our hearts. The sin that nobody sees beneath our "good" external behavior.

Before we further unpack these two types of sin, a quick summary of the parable in Luke 15 that Jesus tells of a father and his two sons:

The younger brother wanted to live free, without the responsibilities of the estate or anyone telling him what to do, so he asked his father for his portion of the inheritance. In that culture this request was equivalent to saying, "I want your money, but I don't want anything to do with you." Not only was it deeply disrespectful, but it warranted the father's disowning him. But the father did as requested and divided the estate between his two sons. The younger son left for a faraway country where he went on to squander his money living recklessly.

Eventually after losing everything and working a lowly job, the younger son awakened to his sin. He made the decision to go back to his father, repent, and beg to serve as hired help. Counter to how one would expect the disrespected patriarch to respond, when the father saw his son in the distance, he was filled with compassion. He did not hold his son's sin against him but ran toward his son, and then threw a huge homecoming celebration. In this father, we see a picture of God's grace toward his wayward children. But there is another storyline here that is often missed—the story of the older brother.

The entire time the younger brother was away, the older brother was at the family property doing what he was supposed to. And when he saw his brother had returned, he did not share his father's joy. In fact, he angrily refused his father's invitation to join the party. But the father affirmed his love for him and left the door open for the older son to come into the party. And that's where the story ends.

Much has been written about this story. For our purposes, I want to focus on the older brother's response to his father's rejoicing over the younger brother's return. It is no small thing that the father, the party's host, had to walk out of the party in an effort to convince the older brother to join in. But the older brother was consumed by jealousy ("you never gave me a young goat") and perhaps also greed (reinstating his young brother as an heir would most likely take from his inheritance). He had served his father faithfully doing everything right and now his undeserving rebellious brother was being celebrated and would get what was rightfully his. That didn't seem fair!

The prideful older brother thought he was more deserving. What was lost on him was his own self-serving motivation for obedience. Did he obey the father out of love or for his own self-ish gain? He wanted the benefits of the father's wealth, so he did the right things, but his heart was far from the father. In this way he was no different from the outwardly disobedient brother; they both only cared about the father's stuff. Ironically, in the end it was the one who knew his sin—the younger brother—who confessed and repented. He knew his need for grace. The elder brother was blind to his need.

All of us (kids included) typically gravitate into either the younger brother or the older brother category of sin. And some days we can be in one category and the next we might be in the other! But either way we bend, we are all in the same sin-sinking boat, in desperate need of the Savior who came to love us and give us grace despite our rebelliousness.

But knowing what category we tend toward and where our children land can be helpful. As categories they expand our view of sin, so we don't fall back on our kids' "good" behavior as the marker of how they are doing. For instance, in Christian circles it is not uncommon to hear someone described as "on fire for the Lord." But the basis for our saying things like this is strictly outward behavior. A better indicator than behavior is what someone does with their sin—do they openly acknowledge that they are sinners who need to repent and turn to Jesus every day? Remember from the last chapter, living redemptively entails dealing honestly with sin.

The foundation to build on with our kids is that Christianity is not about trying to get better and better, or even about being good. It's about seeing we aren't good, which is why we need a Savior. It's about believing God's acceptance of us is based on Jesus's perfection, not ours. When we get this, a funny thing happens—we want to obey him because of what he's done for us. Law-driven Christian teaching leads to hiding behind a mask and faking spirituality, while grace-based Christianity leads to obedience becoming our heart's delight, instead of a duty. Kids who grow up with law-based religiosity frequently fall into the two-thirds of kids who run away from the church as soon as they can.[5]

Likewise, when we are tempted to police our kids' behavior instead of shepherd their hearts, or when we care more about what they look like on the outside than what's going on in the inside, we inadvertently lead them to be older brothers, who in time may grow tired of hiding and swing over to the younger brother camp. Practically speaking, when we deal with our children's issues by sending them to time out, grounding them, or taking away an object or privilege without also addressing their heart all we are doing is punishing bad behavior. We have not fixed anything, although we might have inadvertently encouraged them to figure out how to be sneakier the next time.

There is an alternative way. Don't get me wrong we didn't (and don't) get discipline or parenting right all the time. My kids will tell you! But when our kids were young, we went through the same version of a redemptive conversation every time we disciplined them; you might find it helpful. It went something like this:

> *Parent*: Honey, why did you hide the hair you cut
>   under your stuffed animal?
>
> *Child*: Because I didn't want you to see it.
>
> *Parent*: Why?
>
> *Child*: Because I knew it was wrong?
>
> *Parent*: You knew it was wrong and wanted to hide it
>   from me because you were afraid you would get
>   in trouble?
>
> *Child*: Yes
>
> *Parent*: Adam and Eve did that same thing in the
>   garden. We all try to hide and cover up when
>   we know we've done wrong. Did you know God
>   came for people who try to hide their sin?
>
> *Child*: Yes

Parent: What do we need to do when we realize we've
   sinned?

Child: Ask for forgiveness.

Parent: Yes, and what happens after you ask for
   forgiveness?

Child: Clean slate!

Our daughter would get so excited about the clean slate given to her by God! But keep in mind the responses given here by our daughter didn't just naturally come. We had to diligently teach her truth. (As a related side, a child catechism book is so helpful for this. See the resource list at the end of the book for a recommendation.) Of course, you will want to talk to your child in your own way, but you may find the circular redemptive living diagram from chapter 7 to be a good visual reminder that a redemptive conversation includes these elements: confession, repentance, forgiveness, grace, and restoration.

When redemptive living is our aim, our stance toward one another can be welcoming of confession and not stingy with forgiveness. Furthermore, those in the wrong should not fear confessing sin, but see it as the necessary step for forgiveness, grace, and restoration to run rampant. But honest confession must be really honest, meaning it is not simply saying, "I'm sorry I hurt you." It is acknowledging *specifically* what we did, and how we hurt one another. Apart from hearing this, the other party will likely not experience the offender as repentant and consequently struggle more to give grace.

In our family, because we frequently used the term *clean slate* (another category!), our daughter learned that God's grace and forgiveness was full and complete. With a clean slate there is no need to wallow in shame, beat ourselves up, or try to atone for ourselves. A clean slate does not mean there is no discipline. Even with consequences, the reality of a clean slate enabled our children to know we weren't holding their sin against them, that we were okay with each other.

On the contrary, if we hold their sin against them by referring to it or expressing our continuing disapproval, we communicate a lie about God. God is not like that. Unlike Santa Claus's list of who has been naughty or nice, God doesn't keep a record of wrongs. Our pastor friend Clay Wooten likes to say, the free gift of candy at Halloween is more accurate of who God is than the way we talk about Christmas gifts coming to only those who are "nice." And with the older brother category in mind, can't you see how that philosophy only furthers outward obedience, but not a heart of obedience?

Categories help our children better understand their hearts. And when we live redemptively extending grace, not condemnation to our children, we open the door to more honest conversations. They learn they don't have to pretend. It's okay, encouraged even, to admit their older- or younger-brother tendencies and sin. Same for us—remember we go first.

Questions for Reflection and Discussion:

1. How did this chapter challenge you in your role as primary shepherd of your kids' hearts?
2. Are there categories you've already introduced to your kids even if you hadn't thought of them in this manner before? What new categories do you plan to create?
3. In what ways do you see yourself as either the older brother or the younger brother?
4. How do you see using the older brother/younger brother categories to help your children better understand sin?

Chapter 9
Building a Foundation for Redemptive Conversations

Can you hear it? They're screaming between the lines.
Chase me. Pursue me. Reach out to me.
Notice me. Rescue me. Save me!

— DREW HILL

PARENTS OFTEN ASK me for advice for how to get their kids to talk. Why, they wonder, is it so difficult to have open and honest conversations? Unfortunately, these parents aren't alone; open and safe dialogues within families are not the norm. But from adolescents, I hear that they would be grounded for life if they told their parents certain things they've done. Many kids think that to keep their parents happy they have to hide behind masks and keep playing the Christian game. They are distancing themselves from their parents as they fear rejection should they be found out. Sadly, when our kids don't experience absolute acceptance and love at home, they learn to relate to God in the same way. Hiding from him, living as if under his frown, doubting his love for them.

Along with fear, there are a few other big reasons kids don't openly share with their parents. In fact, the same reasons given by teens in an online survey I conducted before writing my book, *Face Time*, are the same complaints I hear now as a counselor from my adolescent counselees.[1] Here are some of the most common responses:

"I don't trust them."

"They won't understand."

"I don't want them to worry about me."

"We're not close."

"They will judge me."

"They will try to fix me instead of just listening."

"Too awkward to talk about *xyz*."

I know none of us want our own kids to feel any of these sentiments. The good news is there are proactive preventive approaches we can take to help our kids know they can talk to us, not because we told them, "You can tell me anything," but because we've *showed* them. Some of what follows are things we can do to increase open communication; others are things that stop openness dead in it tracks.

But remember that living redemptively with one another as we discussed in the last chapter is the bedrock foundation for each of these ways of bettering our communication. At times we will miss opportunities for connecting and identifying with our children because of our own distractions. We will fail to listen well because of our own agenda or emotional response. We will default back into nagging or inadvertently shaming because of fear and the "need" to control. We will never be the perfect parent.

As I have written previously, parenting is hard and connecting takes work, but God has not left you to yourself. As we seek to draw out our children, God calls us to draw unto him. In our uncertainty and inadequacies, in our fears and weaknesses, in our deepest desires, in our hopes and hopelessness, he calls us to come.[2] For he will "equip you that you may do his will, working in us that which is pleasing in his sight, through Jesus Christ . . ." (Hebrews 13:21). By his strength and because of his grace, our sin and failures can be the catalyst for growing in grace together.

With that said, six ways to move toward our children:

Connection

First and foremost, intentional connecting time is key. We do this when we hold our newborn baby. We look him in the eyes, talk to him, sing to him, feed him, snuggle him tight, without anything else in the world distracting us. But somewhere between toddlerhood and the teenage years, we forget the importance of continued connecting. Looking our child in the eyes. Giving healthy touch to our child. Playing with our child. Giving our undivided attention and simply delighting in our child.

The age of the child will determine what connecting entails. With younger children it may be building blocks, having a tea party, using Play-Doh, or coloring. As they get older, it may be arts and crafts, baking, or playing games. My youngest loves to play chess, so even though he out-strategizes me 99 percent of the time, I keep sitting down to play. Connecting also looks like paying attention to what that particular child loves. Even if you have zero interest in, say, Star Wars or a particular sport or video game, because you love your child, you invest yourself in knowing about and speaking the language of whatever it is he or she is interested in.

This is not rocket science, but in our busy lives we think we are spending time with our kids when really we are multi-tasking and only half there. Or we think we are connecting because we are around our kids, but we are not really *with* them.[3] Instead, we are peppering them with questions, "Did you get your homework done?" "Did you clean your room?" "Did you talk to your teacher about that missing assignment?" Did you, did you, did you, and before we know it, we are in full-out lecture mode and our kids have tuned us out. While such questions have a time and place, I encourage you to dedicate yourself to making true connection a habit. Just ten minutes a day of undistracted connecting goes further than you might imagine for both our little kids and our big kids.[4] For our delight in them is a picture of God's delight in us.

Throughout Scripture we read that God delights in his children—Psalm 18:19, Proverbs 8:31, Isaiah 62:4, to name a few. And as we've talked about, our children learn about who God is based on our model, so when they see us take interest and pleasure in them, it is easier to believe God does the same. That he too delights in them. On the contrary, if we treat our children like they are a burden or a project to perfect, they will fear their standing before God.

Active Listening

I wish I could take back the many times I was only half-hearing one of my children because I was zeroed in on my laptop, in the car caught up in my own thoughts, or distracted by my own to-do list. Consequently, I missed opportunities to engage. Instead of asking follow-up questions, too many times I simply nodded, "Mmm-hmm." If this is our habit by the time kids become teenagers, they will no longer come to us. Without a track record of *really* listening, they will have learned to go elsewhere or to stop sharing altogether.

We must listen not only with our ears, but with our eyes and minds. When our children speak (or remain quiet), notice their body language—what is being "said" that is not being said. Be curious about why they share something, or what they talk frequently about. These observations give us clues as to what occupies their minds, which helps us engage on a deeper level. For example, when one of my sons was a high school freshman, he told me several of his friends were spending the night together. I took this in strictly as information and responded along the lines of, "Oh, that's fun." What I completely missed was my son felt left out. His friends were together, and he hadn't been included. Had I looked up from my phone or engaged my mind a bit more, I might I have realized what he was *really* saying.

Quite often the words that come out of our kids' mouths only scratches the surface of what is going on in their heads and in their hearts. To get underneath, we must *actively* listen. Active listening includes paying attention to what you see, rephrasing what you hear, and asking probing questions.

Making observations includes noticing differences in appearance or behaviors, such as fatigue, fidgeting, or diverted eyes, that offer nonverbal cues to follow up on. Rephrasing is simply stating back to your child in your own words what you heard him/her say. For instance, if my child said, "I slept terrible last night." I would say back, "You had a bad night's sleep." In doing so I am not adding any new content but when your child (or any person) hears back what was said it often leads to elaboration. At the very least it helps the individual feel heard.

Probing questions are not yes/no questions, and they may not even be a question at all. One of my favorite phrases to use is, "Tell me more." The goal in using probing questions is to get more information, yes, but information that leads to a better understanding of your child's inner person. For your sake and his or hers.

This is what counselors do, but parents, you can do it even better! You know your child in a way that a counselor doesn't. Not only does your intimate knowledge and front row seat to your child's life give you a leg up, but don't forget, *you* are the number one influencer in your child's life. God has given them into our care (James 1:17) and we are to be a good steward of them (1 Corinthians 4:2), which includes faithfully seeking to draw them out. In hearing and knowing your child, you build a stronger connection, and *you* get to be the shaping instrument you are called to be in the life of your child.

No Nagging

Along with lecturing and passive listening, nagging has a way of quickly silencing our kids. Moms especially have a hard time grasping this. We seem to be hardwired toward it, but if you trace the nagging backward, do you not find the idol of control? And if there is anything moms want, is it not control? When we nag, though, we convey to our kids they aren't enough.

As I've told you it wasn't until my daughter was a high school senior that I learned that my nagging made my daughter feel like a failure. By trying to control outcomes, I was crippling her. And the more I tried to control, the more she pushed away from me. I understand now why she didn't want to share with me, or even be around me—why open herself up to extra stress and more critique?

Our unchecked idols hurt our kids and hinder our relationships with them. That is why in this book and in counseling I start with us—the parents. It is easy to point our fingers at our kids, but we must look inward first to see where our idolatrous desires and behaviors are pushing and prodding them. My nagging was the outward expression of my real issue—falsely believing my security and rest was dependent on my ordered control as opposed to trusting the One who rules over all (Psalm 22:28; Colossians 1:17).

No Shaming

Recently when driving by my kids' former middle school, my daughter told me that seeing the parking lot next door to the school where parents parked to wait for their carpools, reminds her of a particular middle school friend, who would make out with her boyfriend right in the open where all the parents could see. She and her other friends worried that if their moms saw this, they would think that they were being badly influenced, and would not be allowed to hang out with this girl.

Though I never saw the described incident, my daughter and her friends were not wrong in their fears. We parents are prone to snap judgments. We falsely assume, because one person or teens in general are involved in a bad behavior, that everyone must be doing *xyz*. We then label certain individuals as "bad" and ban our kids from them. But I've learned, even if our kids are embarrassed by someone's behavior, they sure don't want Mom and Dad to judge their friend. Their friendships reflect upon them, so to judge one of their friends is to judge them.

Consider how you have responded when you have learned something, or your child has shared something bad about a classmate, and how it may have led them to be more careful about what they share. Now consider, your response to your child when he or she has does something wrong.

Do you freak out? Show shock? Throw out law-based phrases like one of these:

"How could you?"

"What were you thinking?"

"You should have never been hanging out with them."

"What will people think?"

When we do, we act as if we aren't fellow sinners living in a broken world, that we would *never* do something so bad. Consequently, instead of creating a safe place to share, instead of helping our kids process their heart motives, instead of lovingly leading our kids to repentance, our shock fills our kids with more shame than they already feel.

Shame is connected to the law. It started in the garden after Adam and Eve ate the fruit. Attempting to cover their nakedness and shame, they hid. It was their failure to measure up to God's law: "You shall not eat of the fruit of the tree that is in the midst of the garden" (Genesis 3:3). Ever since, shame is part of our human experience. Therefore, anything internally or externally that leads us to feel or exposes our not-enoughness—our inadequacies—creates shame.

As parents we must learn to put on a poker face. Because when we repetitively over-respond, shame is heightened, and our kids default to hiding their sin. Then they stop telling us what is going on with them and their friends. But when we restrain our own emotions, we open the door to further conversation. We also open the door to grace-based parenting with an aim at heart transformation as opposed to law and behavioral modification. I realize that staying calm is not always easy. When we do, I credit it to the intervening work of the Holy Spirit. When we don't, we have an opportunity to repent and ask God to help us live more dependently on him.

Identifying

We must learn to get in the boat with our kids. By this I mean, identify with them—in their emotions, worries, struggles, and sin. Help them see that we too are human and get what they are going through. Even if we don't "get" it exactly or maybe haven't experienced what they are dealing with, when we move beyond the external behaviors and circumstances to the heart, we discover how alike we really are. We might be in different boats, but we are in the same choppy waters because, "For all have sinned and fall short of the glory of God" (Romans 3:23).

When one of my children was in middle school, we learned this child had a vape. We could have responded with shock over doing something wrong. Certainly, this child would have learned to be sneakier. We could have strictly grounded this child, but punishment alone would have done nothing to change the heart. Instead, we asked probing questions. What we discovered is that the reason for the vaping was to fit in. Smoking with peers made this child feel accepted and cool.

I get that. I want to be accepted by others. I want to feel cool. Boom! That was the entry point. Because we could identify on a heart-level with the same idolatrous desires, we had a fruitful conversation that day. There were still consequences but none of the ostracizing or shame that often accompanies discipline. And because this child saw us in the same boat as fellow sinners, we have continued to have ongoing open dialogue.

Normalizing Taboo Topics

Last, we must normalize taboo topics. We can't expect kids to come to us with their questions when we have not initiated certain awkward topics. What if a kid is struggling with temptation to sexual sin, will he come to Mom and Dad? Not if sex is not something freely talked about it. But it doesn't have to be this way. Here is the difference:

One evening my husband and I were with a group of nearly empty-nester friends when the conversation drifted to our collective fears related to college-aged kids, specifically the hookup culture so prevalent on college campuses. While one of the dads shared with us what he told his sons about sexual temptation, one of our teenage boys came downstairs into the room where we were gathered. The conversation continued, but with the boy now listening in, a few moms began squirming and asked that we change the subject. This boy was not their son. His parents were unfazed by his presence, and he himself didn't act embarrassed or make any move to excuse himself. He was also eighteen.

The scenario was telling of the types of conversations that are acceptable and discussed in each home. Clearly sex was an off-limits topic for the parents who felt uncomfortable by a teenager's presence among us. But for the family whose son was in the room, the topic wasn't one to shut down or avoid.

When kids hear only law pertaining to awkward topics, such as, "You better not have sex," the message they receive is "sex is bad." Consequently, if they have thoughts about sex or engage in it, they believe they are bad and will hide in shame. Therefore, in addition to habitually initiating heart-level theological conversations, we must also normalize conversations about taboo topics.

For if we don't lead the way into these conversations, someone else will become our children's go-to source. We are the ones who are to train up our children (Ephesians 6:4). Failure to do so in this area, as in all others, leaves our children more vulnerable to the ways of the world, putting culture, not the Bible, in position to steer our kids' views about sex and gender.

On the other hand, if from the time our kids are young, we start talking at age-appropriate levels about sex and other hard issues, they learn that these are things they can go to Mom and Dad with, as the boy, who continued to stand in on our "adult" conversation, knew. Likewise, because my husband and I both participated in the initial and ongoing sex talks with our daughter and sons, conversations including the words *penis*, *pornography*, and *oral sex*, as well as complaints about periods, happen at our dinner table. Exactly what I wanted—for both sexes to feel comfortable, whether with Mom, Dad, or siblings, to talk about anything.

I will add that in today's culture, Christian parents don't have a choice to not talk about sex and gender issues if we want to shape a healthy, biblical foundation for our children. Scripture calls us to be "wise as serpents and innocent as doves" (Matthew 10:16), which is to say we must not be naive and yet we are called to innocence. Our kids need to know God's design for marriage and good intent for sex. When kids grow up learning about the good gift of sex in marriage, they see it as something worth protecting for their future spouse. When they hear nothing, they are far less likely to wait for marriage. When all they hear is, "Don't do it," they will more likely feel shame surrounding the enjoyment of sex even once they are married.

Just as one of the reasons we don't initiate spiritual conversations is feeling ill-equipped, the same is true with the ever-changing culture narratives about sex and gender, pornography, social media, and the like. Honestly, it is hard to keep up. But please don't put your head in the sand. Listed in appendix B (page 155) are a few of my favorite go-to resources to help with these topics, along with other resources mentioned in this book.

More importantly, in your struggle to navigate these topics and know what to say and how to engage with your kids, remember you are not alone. God is with you. Turn to him in prayer, telling him your worries and fears (Philippians 4:6–7). Seek his wisdom (James 1:5). And be encouraged that he will provide for all of your needs and, by his power at work within you, he will enable you to step into the challenging conversations (Philippians 4:19). As I have mentioned before, my anthem verse in parenting is, "When I am weak, he is strong" (2 Corinthians 12:10). Remind yourself often that in your insufficiency, his power, his strength, and his grace abound (2 Corinthians 12:9)!

Questions for Reflection and Discussion:

1. In what ways have you helped or hindered your children from talking honestly and openly with you?
2. What, if any, changes did this chapter challenge you to implement in your family? Have you made any biblical connections that encourage you in moving toward your children?
3. Multiple verses were referenced throughout the chapter. Take some time to go back and look some, or all, of these up. I encourage you then to make a list or write some out to keep as a quick guide when you go to God in prayer.

Chapter 10
Family Rhythms

A culture will be created by default, so we are wise
to consider what culture we are creating.

— KRISTA GILBERT

IF YOU'VE EVER been curious about what someone (or you!) values most, there is no better way to start than to look at how time and money are spent. "For where your treasure is, there your heart will be also" (Matthew 6:21). Now we would likely all agree that apart from a relationship with Christ, family is our number one treasure. But I wonder if an honest assessment of our time and finances would show this to be functionally true. For amid our busy schedules and the pressures and values of our culture, prioritizing what we say means most to us doesn't always align with what we are actually doing. Often our family time, church involvement, and friendships suffer under the pressure attending to jobs, kids' activities, and hobbies. Sometimes our first loves even take a backseat to the pursuit of appearance, success, perfection, happiness, comfort. Back to our idols you see!

Sin is sneaky. We don't set out to elevate jobs or hobbies over our people. We certainly wouldn't say we care more about our appearance or comfort than our children. But at times this is just what happens; I know I've been guilty of investing more energy into various projects than intentional parenting and I've been more bent on "checking out" than showing love to my children.

While we could justify that sometimes our jobs leave us no choice, or that we all need downtime, still we must start with *our* hearts.

If we rightly understand human depravity, we know that "the heart is deceitful above all things, and desperately sick" (Jeremiah 17:9). That means we are prone to idol worship and doing things that betray what we say we believe. In our delusion, we elevate the temporal over the eternal. We lose sight of what God's Word tell us is true. Like Adam and Eve who saw the fruit and believed the lie about what it would offer, we get caught up in the world's ways.

We think we must follow the script handed to us otherwise we'll get left behind. Consequently, we jump on the hamster wheel, believing if we do all the "right" things we will find a life of success for our families. But we don't have to live that way. We really do have a choice. We *can* slow down and say no without disengaging from the world all together. And we must set boundaries for our families and kids while also teaching our kids to set their own. "Do not be conformed to this world, but be transformed by the renewal of your mind, that by testing you may discern what is the will of God, what is good and acceptable and perfect" (Romans 12:2).

We can't go off feelings, desires, or public opinion; the mind is where the battle takes place. But for the mind to be transformed, we need the continual influence of the gospel. Ongoing, all the time, we need to be reminded of Christ's work and worth for us. For a desire to live transformed, set apart from the world, different, in a manner honoring of him, comes not by me telling you to, or from hearing more law, but out of delight for who Christ is for you. Same with our kids, which we will discuss more under boundaries.

Our desires and priorities change only when we are more under the influence of Christ than culture. To this end, we will look at three interrelated areas of transformed living: slowing down, saying no, and setting limits. As we do, keep Paul's words to the Corinthians in mind, "And we all, with unveiled face, beholding the glory of the Lord, are being transformed into the same image from one degree of glory to another. For this comes from the Lord who is the Spirit" (2 Corinthians 3:18). In other words, as we fix our eyes on Christ, the Spirit at work within us reshapes our affections and remakes us more in Christ's likeness.

Slowing Down

With one of my children now married and two in college, I've seen how fast the years really do go by. I miss the games and activities, but even more I miss being under one roof—sitting down at the dinner table, playing games, watching a TV series, relaxing by the pool. I miss worshipping together and discussing the sermon over Sunday lunch. I miss the laughter and noise.

It is in these moments of casual, everyday normal life where we lay foundations and build connection that shape our kids for a lifetime. But how can we if we are never home together? If all our time is scheduled? Therefore, we must *proactively* think through what prioritizing family time looks like, including how we will guard our time.

What will you do early on to create an environment, and instill in your kids a desire to be with family? To foster sibling relationships?

How will you lead your kids to love the Lord? To make faith their own?

What will you say no to? What will you insist on?

We didn't do this right all the time. But we did have some nonnegotiables in place, one being Sunday morning church. Now some people have said to me, "Well, your husband is a pastor. You have to go to church. It is easy for you." My response is twofold. First, church is a value, not because of my husband's profession, but because God ordained church as the institution in which his people are to gather to hear his Word and grow together. Therefore, as believers we are committed to our local body despite my husband's profession. Consequently, we made the decision that competitive travel team sports were not something we could participate in. One of my sons did play on a competitive baseball team with local-area weekend tournaments, but from the beginning we let the coach know he would not be able to play in any Sunday morning games.

Second, ministry families struggle in the same ways as everyone else. There are mornings I don't necessarily feel like going to church and mornings my children don't either. My children grew up in a church plant without many, if any, peers which meant church wasn't always "fun." But through their unique experiences they gained an understanding of the church that precludes the consumer mindset common to how we approach church today.

Another nonnegotiable was downtime at home—without friends. For the health of our family as well as our kids' need for unscheduled rest, we did not always allow our kids to make plans simply because they were free. We did get pushback. Our kids did not always like our decisions, but there is always another social event. Don't fall for the lie that if your kid misses out, he or she will be detrimentally affected or excluded. And they won't hate you even if they are mad at you for a bit. Usually, despite my kids' initial complaints, they ended up content with a night at home with the family.

Always allowing them to be on the go can adversely affect the development of sibling bonding. When our daughter was a teenager and her brothers still young enough that she found them annoying, the last thing she wanted to do was hang with them or go watch their games. I regret that we didn't insist then that she support her brothers more in their endeavors or encourage her to spend time with them in the same way we had when they were younger. Fast-forward to her freshman year in college, missing out on their lives became her biggest regret, and "sibling night" her favorite thing when she came home. Sibling night often included going for a drive and out for ice cream. The boys looked up to her more than she knew. Today, they frequently call and text each other for all sorts of advice and to just share life.

If you're kids fight now, know it is not necessarily indicative of the future. There is hope, even when you feel you have fallen short in helping them develop relationships separate from you. Give yourself grace and ask God for his help in changing course. If their sibling relationships are a challenge, continue to do what you can trusting that in God's time he will grow the relationships between your children.

Saying No

We are prone to justify our participation in kids' sports and activities as together time. Now I realize I may step on some toes here, so please hear me—I am for kids' sports and activities. We are a HUGE sports family, I already told you there was a time one of our sons was pursuing collegiate football. I also believe that supporting our children in their endeavors is incredibly important. But sitting in the stands with our kids on the field or court or in the pool isn't equivalent to quality family time. Likewise, riding in the car to and from activities and tournaments can be a catalyst to quality family time, but not when the kids are sleeping, listening to music through their own earbuds, or reading, which is often the case. At least in our car! So just because we are together does not mean we are connecting.

Speaking as a counselor now (not a parent), I have counselees with parents who drove them to practices and traveled with them to tournaments weekend after weekend who not only feel disconnected from their parents but feel loved only for their performance. They report rarely sitting down at home for dinner together or having meaningful conversation because they were always on the go. They couldn't go to church because again they were on the go. Lacking a foundation of *Christ is life* because, functionally, the sport was life (and the teen's identity), many of these adolescents and young adults struggle to know their worth. Many of the siblings of those playing the sport the family's life revolved around also struggle with identity and worth. They report feeling neglected, less than, and bitter.

When we make the decisions to join a club sport, usually we don't see where it could lead. We may imagine it ending with a collegiate scholarship, but we don't see at what cost the dividing and conquering between moms and dads, the pressure to perform, single-minded focus, and lack of church involvement will have on individual family members and the family as a whole. All we see is what everyone else is doing which creates a fear in us that, if we don't do the same, our children will miss out on future opportunities.

Likewise, when we make decisions to go to the lake for the weekend or allow Saturday night plans and spend-the-nights to circumvent church attendance, it may not seem like a big deal on occasion, but it can be a slippery slope. One time leads to a child saying, "But you let me last time," or us justifying our decision by saying, "We'll watch a sermon online." But if this becomes our habit, we communicate that faith is not as important as our personal pursuits and fun. I don't intend to communicate legalism about church attendance. Making it to every church service is not the be-all and end-all. The point is, for better or worse, little decisions add up over time. Therefore, sometimes we need to say NO.

Regardless of the circumstance, I know it can be hard at times to say no. Especially when your child pulls the "no one else's parents make them leave early" or "everybody else is going" cards. Believe me, I've been there! But from my experience, as I shared in the first chapter, when your children learn your no means no, you make it easier on yourself, and your kids. Unpredictability and wavering convictions confuse our kids and lead to more ongoing arguments.

Setting Boundaries

When my daughter was in high school, we had many arguments about curfew. Not just the set time of it but the fact she even had curfew. Apparently, we were the only ones (lol!), so imagine my surprise after her first semester of college when she thanked me for imposing a curfew!

She realized what we had said all along was actually true—"We love you too much not to do what we can to keep you safe." But it took hearing from some new friends whose parents didn't give them curfews that she was actually the "lucky" one. The way they saw it, our daughter had parents who loved and cared for her enough to set limits. They on the other hand felt unloved by the lack of protection.

Here are some questions I've heard from kids about their parents:

Did they care more about being the cool parent than they did about my well-being?

Did they not consider the harm that could come from hanging out with the opposite sex and drinking late at night?

Did they not love me enough to say no?

Even when kids clamor for freedom and want to be their own authority, they want boundaries. First and foremost, boundaries communicate love. Boundaries also offer structure, protection, and guidance, all of which are necessary to help them flourish and grow. I like the analogy I once heard that compared boundaries to a fish tank. The fish might think of the tank as restrictive, but without the glass walls keeping the fish in, the water would spill out and the fish would die.

When our children are young, boundaries seem obvious. But many parents withdraw when children get older and start bucking up against them. We fall for some of the worldly lies mentioned in chapter 5 or fall prey to idols. Parents, please, be the parent. We would never allow them as youngsters to run out in the street, but allowing a free for all with technology (to use just one example) is equally dangerous.

Believe it or not, more teenagers than you might expect have told me they have wanted their parents to intervene with boundaries, to tell them no. One teenager I know even told me she snuck out deliberately with the hope her parent would lay down the law, so she knew she was loved. Another teenager shared feeling trapped in the group she was hanging out with and the behavior they were engaging in, but without any limitations put forth by her parents, stepping away was too hard for her to do one her own.

I often also hear parents speak of not wanting to impose their beliefs on their children, but to let their children make up their own minds—not just about religious beliefs, but gender and sex, and morality in general. This is one reason we now have young children and adolescents making life-altering decisions about their bodies. Even from a secular standpoint we should see that giving free rein and decision-making authority to children whose brains are not fully developed is not loving.

Our children need us to speak into *all* the difficult topics and set boundaries. Let's just take sex for instance. It is not enough for you to hope they won't have sex before marriage. Start the ongoing conversation about sex and God's good design as early as possible. As they become teens, continue the conversations but also set practical boundaries to help guard against sexual sin. They need you to enter in with wisdom, instruction, and guardrails!

But again, when it comes to boundaries, we must examine our idols. And not just those parents who flounder or fail to give boundaries, but also overparenting parents driven to lay down too much law. We can teeter in either direction depending on what rules our hearts. On one end of the spectrum, we want our children to experience fun. In doing so we may hope to keep the peace and be more like a best friend. Or we want to live vicariously through them. On the other end of the spectrum, we are so full of fear that we place rigid restrictions on everything. But when we try to control their safety, morality, beliefs, relationships, or anything and everything else we unknowingly place our trust in "law" or the rules to work in our children's hearts in a way that only the Spirit can do. Unfortunately, as we've discussed, law-driven parenting with an emphasis on performance-based commands (dos and don'ts) which we intend to keep kids from sinning, often leads to resentment and rebellion.

When my husband was a campus minister at a large Christian university, we noticed that frequently the kids who strayed furthest from God (at least for a time) were those who had grown up in the most restricted and sheltered environments. They had lived under rigid boundaries (law) and tended to view God as a policeman out to bust them. Because these kids didn't feel like they could have honest conversations with their parents, they hid what they were up to and lived dual lifestyles. All the while, they were riddled with shame which is what led them to flee from the church as soon as they gained their freedom.

Sadly, these students' experiences led to an inaccurate view of God. They didn't "get" that in Christ there is no condemnation (Romans 8:1). Functionally they didn't believe that in Christ, there is no reason to fear, as "fear has to do with punishment," but "perfect love casts out fear" (1 John 4:18). Jesus did not come to condemn the world but to save the world through *his* perfect obedience and love for sinners (John 3:17)!

But law-driven Christianity is all about meeting a perfect (yet unattainable) standard on our own. Under law-driven parenting, good outward behavior is synonymous with inward obedience. On the other hand, a gospel-centered, grace-based parenting seeks to help our kids believe better, not behave better. In other words, the focus is on leading kids to see their need for Jesus. Knowing that they will sin, a greater emphasis is placed on what to do with our sin. And the more we know our sin, the greater our affection for the one who dealt mercifully for us in our sin, which in turn, leads us to want to live obediently to him. By no means is grace-based parenting equivalent to no boundaries or consequences. That would not be grace at all! Boundaries are necessary and loving, as is discipline, when given properly. In other words, grace-based parenting is parenting with the overall good of the child in mind, not just the outward "right" behavior or opinion of other as the measuring stick. But as author and licensed counselor Julie Lowe writes, "Rules without connection and rapport result in children who see their parents (and Christ) as distant, authoritarian, unloving, and impersonal. The reverse may be true as well. . . . Kids instinctively sense that a parent who doesn't give them rules does not love them."[1]

When we try to impose rules as a dictator, it just doesn't fly. That's why I don't care for the "because I said so" response when children question us. Rather, when they ask us why, instead of feeling annoyed or inconvenienced let's see it as an opportunity to shepherd. Take this scenario for example:

Your daughter wants a certain clothing item that is much too revealing. You say no and may even add a "because I said so" when she questions. Or you tell her, "It's inappropriate." Either way these responses do nothing to lovingly shepherd her. Instead take the opportunity to talk to her about modesty, as well as what is going in our hearts when we want to dress in revealing ways (think idolatry!). When this is the conversation, you take it to the heart-level and bring the gospel in.

You have also engaged in relationship building, which is key. Children who don't feel close to their parents have a harder time submitting to their rules. They need to know you are *for* them. Most of us probably think it should be obvious to our children that we are for them. But they need to hear your words match your actions. Love is often spelled T-I-M-E. Having your attention, affection, and interest is what gives weight to your words and helps them feel loved. Then, within the context of a close relationship (close according to how they experience it), even when your child doesn't like or agree with your rules, he or she more readily accepts your God-given authority.

As for the actual boundaries we set, since there is no parenting formula to follow, different families will come to different conclusions about particular rules and boundaries that are all still God-honoring. The Bible gives us that leeway in many areas. But we do know from Scripture that God gave boundaries for the good of his people from the beginning.

> The LORD God took the man and put him in the garden of Eden to work it and keep it. And the LORD God commanded the man, saying, "You may surely eat of every tree of the garden, but of the tree of the knowledge of good and evil you shall not eat, for in the day that you eat of it you shall surely die." (Genesis 2:15–17)

We also see throughout Scripture there are two ways of living—the way of the righteous who follow God's law and the way of the wicked, or foolish, who disregard God's instruction. As parents, it is our responsibility to train up our children (Proverbs 22:6) to know the way of the Lord. Giving boundaries with instruction is a huge part of that training. To help you navigate the ins and outs of setting boundaries in your household, I have listed some questions for you to consider. My hope is these questions will solidify your resolve for boundary-setting while also steering you to evaluate your motives before setting certain boundaries. To this end use these questions as a litmus for whatever boundary issue is at hand.

What does God's Word say about this issue?

By setting this boundary, what do I hope to accomplish?

Is a boundary necessary for my child's physical, emotional, mental, and/or spiritual well-being?

Is the reason I am imposing or not imposing a boundary being influenced by an idol of mine?

What teaching time or conversation needs to happen alongside this boundary?

Am I setting clear expectations surrounding the boundary?

How can I maintain consistency with this boundary?

That last question about consistency is crucial. When we aren't consistent, our children don't know what to expect and become confused. They also learn that we don't mean what we say so they take advantage of getting around our rules. Consistency creates security and helps them develop the courage to hold tight to their own boundaries.

Let's just play this out. A child whose parents inconsistently uphold boundaries receives mixed messages. Sometimes it seems okay to do something, other times it is not. Another child has parents who are very clear in their instruction surrounding boundaries and consistent in upholding them. Fast-forward to the teen years when these now adolescent children are confronted with peer pressure to engage in sexual activity. Which one do you think is more likely to hold a firm resolve to stick to their boundaries?

As you probably guessed, the child who learned clear firm boundaries will be better equipped to stand firm in her own boundaries, including body boundaries when she is older. Our children learn from what is modeled even more from what we say. Therefore, setting and sticking to our boundaries is one of the most loving, teachable ways to shepherd your child.

But regardless of how your habits of setting and enforcing boundaries, saying no, guarding family time, and otherwise proactively engaging has gone, you have a God whose grace always exceeds our failures. He who set a boundary in the beginning for Adam and Eve, and who gave the Ten Commandments through Moses to his people because he loved them and wanted their best, also gave up his only Son for these same people who did not follow his command. Jesus perfectly kept God's law *for you* so now God sees you only according to his grace. May you feel his smile upon you. May you live in light of it.

Questions for Reflection and Discussion:

1. What priorities do my time/our family's commitments/ finances/relationship reflect? How does this match up or not match up with what we say is most valuable?

2. What small decisions can I trace forward to see how they could lead to challenges down the road? (For example, in chapter 1 we had the mother at the park who gave in to her child's demand for another snack, and years later her daughter had learned how to wear Mom down to get what she wanted.)

3. Use the set of italicized questions in the Setting Boundaries section to evaluate a boundary you have set in place or are considering setting in place. For example, boundaries surrounding screen time.

4. Spend some time in prayer asking God for his help and discernment surrounding time, decisions, and boundary-setting issues in your family.

Chapter 11
Growing in Grace

Our relationships in the family are not about living up to each other's expectations. They are about accepting one another and reflecting God's grace to each other as we are being transformed by the power of the gospel.

— SUSAN HUNT

WHILE I WAS working on this chapter, I also attended a week-long training for counselors. Written everywhere around the building—on the windows, walls, mirrors, and the sweatshirts worn by staff—were the words, "Seen, Heard, Valued." These words, I quickly surmised, were the heartbeat of the host organization, a nonprofit assisting victims of early childhood trauma and breathing life into those whose life experiences have left them feeling unseen, unheard, and not valued.

Both secular and Christian counseling-related books affirm that whether or not a person feels seen, heard, and valued shapes how one sees himself, others, and the world. I see evidence of this every day in the counseling room: adolescents and adults alike who struggle to know their worth because at some point in their lives (often over a long period of time) they absorbed direct and indirect messaging like, "You're not enough," "You're not important," "You're not worth my love or time," "You aren't valuable," "You're uninteresting," "You're a burden," or something similar.[1]

Sometimes those who struggle to know their worth did have loving parents who unknowingly created or contributed to a false narrative. As parents we don't always have the words to express the extent of our love of our children. But because of our own past experiences, preoccupations, stress, and/or idols, we sometimes send wrong messages without realizing it to the people we love most. Sadly, looking back over my two decades of parenting, I know I have.

I wish I had been more aware of how my sin, distractions, and careless words affected my kids. Maybe then I would have pulled away from my laptop or phone when one of my children was trying to talk to me. Maybe then I would've played the game they wanted to play instead of kicking back in my favorite chair in front of the television. Maybe then I would have been more patient when the story they told took too long. Maybe then I would have died to myself more readily instead of expressing my frustration when one of my kids was "too needy." Or, maybe not—even our best intentions are riddled with sin. "For I have the desire to do what is right, but not the ability to carry it out" (Romans 7:18).

Whether we were aware of our sinful responses or not, we can beat ourselves up all day over the should have, would have, could haves, and often we do. And in our guilt and shame, we can convince ourselves that one mistake or failure deems us a bad parent or will doom our child forever. Very quickly this mindset can spiral us down into our own puddle of worthlessness. Just where Satan wants us—inwardly consumed with similar false narratives that our children struggle with—that we aren't good enough, don't measure up, or lack value because of our imperfect performance.

But Christ! We must look up and outside of ourselves to remember:

- First, we are deeply loved. God does not hold our sin against us (Jeremiah 31:34).
- Second, we are also clothed in Christ's righteous robes, which means God sees us as he sees his son— perfect, holy, and righteous (2 Corinthians 5:21).
- Third, God uses even sin to accomplish his good purposes in those he loves (Romans 8:28).

Why then can we not give ourselves grace? Why do we hold ourselves to a standard of perfection?

Functionally, we live as if Christ's finished work wasn't enough. That grace seems too good to be true. Though we may reject works-based theology, we live as if we need to earn our way, that we need to be "good enough" to merit God's love. But what even is good enough? The standards we impose on ourselves, and others, constantly change. The world, social media, and the people in our everyday worlds may give us unrealistic expectations and leave us feeling like we fall short.

Isn't that where "mom guilt" comes from? And fathers have "dad guilt" too. We see what others are doing—somehow seeming to perfectly balance work-life, marriage, parenting, all while maintaining beautiful appearances and an impeccable home— and we feel less than, like we must do more and do better at it all. And don't we place these same expectations on our kids? We see someone else's son working on his Eagle Scout badges, playing piano, a sport, going to Wednesday night church, all while maintaining all As, and all of the sudden we nag at our own kids about doing more and doing better.

What an exhausting way to live! No wonder we as a culture, including our kids, are so stressed out. Imagine with me, then, the difference if instead we lived—truly lived—under Christ's perfection for us. Let's just tease out what might change:

- We would rest in his perfection, his performance, for us (Hebrews 10:14).
- We would be free to confess our sin and failures both to God and others without fear (1 John 1:9; James 5:16).
- We would boast in our weakness instead of trying to make ourselves great (2 Corinthians 12:9).
- We would live loved, knowing his smile upon us even in our sin (Romans 5:8).
- We could appreciate what we see in others without feeling like it indicts us (Romans 12:6; Ephesians 4:7).

Living in this manner is the exact opposite of works righteousness; it is living according to grace. The more we come to see it is all Jesus—his work, his righteousness—the more we will be affected by grace and give grace to others.

For not only is it by grace that we are covered for our failures, but it is by grace that we are able to live in a manner worthy of the gospel. It is grace that we desire to be in God's Word and are influenced by his Word. It is by grace that we bear the fruit of the Spirit—love, joy, peace, patience, kindness, goodness, faithfulness, gentleness, and self-control (Galatians 5:22). Grace is a gift.

Why am I emphasizing this?

Grace changes how we see and respond to everything. For when I "get" grace, I understand that, apart from God's grace at work, our human inclination is self, not godliness. Growing in grace is a lifelong journey. Notice: growing in grace, not perfection! That means some days I'll get it right and sometimes I won't. When I don't, it does not mean I'm going backward. More telling than my sin is what I do with sin.

Do I run to Jesus? Do I confess and repent? Or, do I try to feign victory and perfection?

Growing in Grace

The theological term for a lifetime of growing in grace is *sanctification*. Although we talked about this earlier in the book, I want to revisit it again as we close. If you recall, sanctification is God's shaping and molding process of conforming us more and more into his image.

Beginning with our salvation, when we are made right with God (justified), until we are united with Christ (glorification), we are being sanctified. The sanctification process is not always about getting better and better. It doesn't mean constant victory or that we stop sinning. Growth in the Christian life is more about growing in our need of Jesus than it is about performing better. Yet, as we grow in our awareness of sin and our need for a Savior, our desires to live in a manner worthy of him increase. Evidence of our sanctification may be that we are quicker to seek forgiveness when we sin, or that we have more compassion toward someone we used to have little patience for, or that we are less self-focused.

Each sanctification journey will look different, so we can't compare. Each of us are exactly where God has us in the process right now. This concept can be hard to swallow. I mean how many times have you said to yourself, "I shouldn't still be doing this. I should be better by now!" Or, what about with your kids? How upset do you get when they continue to sin in the same ways? "You should know better than that," we yell!

On one hand, yes, it seems they (or we) should have conquered *it* (whatever *it* is) by now, yet sometimes God leaves us in our sin and struggles. Why God would allow us to continue in our sin doesn't make sense to us. But in his sovereign purposes, he allows ongoing sin in our lives as part of his sanctifying work in us, and in others. That's right—our sanctification is never disconnected from others. God will use the struggles and sin in one's person's life to grow and change another. Nowhere is this clearer than in families.

As a counselor, I like to use the analogy of a mobile hanging over a baby's crib to help counselees see how one family member's action affects the whole. When a baby laying in his crib lightly swats at one object on the mobile, it shakes a bit. But then he gives a big whack and the entire mobile wildly orbits. This is what happens in a family because of sin and trial. The experience and repercussions don't just happen to the one individual, but to everyone in the family. Everyone in a family is connected, so what happens to one, affects all other family members. The church family works the same way. God's sanctifying work within the context of family and relationships is all part of his redemptive plan.

In my own family, through marriage and parenting, I see how God has used conflict, trials, and sin (both big and small) as sanctifying agents in each of our lives. In fact, I would even say one of the most predominant times of growing in grace for me, if not the most predominant time of growth, has been during the parenting teen years. Unlike any other time, I truly had to wrestle with God's sovereignty and my insufficiency and need. Whether with circumstances as overwhelming as my daughter's long, hard eating disorder recovery or with ongoing fears surrounding things such as weekend plans, teenage drivers, student elections, sports, friendships, and grades, my idol of control became glaring. But in my helplessness and need, I came more to the end of myself where all I could do was cry out to him. And it was in that condition that he opened my eyes to see that is exactly where he wants us. "For when I am weak, then I am strong" (2 Corinthians 12:10).

In my weakness and need, particularly in the suffering our family went through with the eating disorder journey, I felt very alone. I knew God was with us, but I didn't feel like others understood. This time of loneliness and sorrow was also not outside of God's sanctifying work in my life. He used it to help me see, really see, others in their suffering, and to grow in compassion for others in their sin and brokenness and trials. I can also say that though I had written one book already, the suffering in our family from the eating disorder is what led to writing my second book, *Face Time*, speaking more to parents, and ultimately returning to school for a counseling degree. So, while I would not wish an eating disorder on anyone or anyone's family, I see God's hand in using it in my life, as he did in my daughter's.

Cultivating Compassion

In talking about sanctification, you may have caught this, but I would be remiss if I did not call your attention directly to the fact that sanctification happens to you. It is a passive condition. "For by a single offering he has perfected for all time *those who are being sanctified*" (Hebrews 10:14, emphasis added).

We are not the actors—God is. It is his doing, on his time-line. My hope therefore is you would stop beating yourself up over every sin. That you would see that God uses even your fail-ures for good. When you neglect to attentively meet your child's every need, you don't have to fear you have messed up your child forever. By no means does this mean we excuse sin, but it should free us to deal honestly—redemptively—with it.

Furthermore, I hope growing in grace leads to you being an agent of grace in the lives of your kids. As parents we often feel personally affronted when our kids do something wrong, espe-cially when it's the same thing for what seems like the millionth time. But their repetitive sin doesn't mean that the last time they said they wouldn't do it again they weren't sincere, just look at yourself! When you see that you too struggle to put certain sins to rest, that you too do the things you don't want, that you too lack the power to not give into a particular temptation, not to mention when you take into account their developmental stage, it should lead to great compassion.

Again, not excusing sin, but if your believing child is being sanctified as you are, they too are being acted upon. God is using circumstances in their lives, and YOU as the primary shaping influence to grow them in grace, in his timing. And when your child who has not made a confession of faith continues sinning, we remember that, at this point in their lives, they do not have the contrary influence of the Spirit and can have compassion on them in their sin.

So, what does this look like? Instead of blasting our kids over their sin, we enter in with gentleness and grace. Now I know, depending on what we are talking about, staying calm can be nearly impossible. We need Christ to be strong for us (or calm in this case) because we are weak. Practically, we may need to walk away and ground ourselves before engaging with our kids.

From a brain science perspective, when you are emotionally charged your child's amygdala detects danger which sends your child into flight, flight, or freeze. In their own high alert state, neither they, nor you, will be able to access the prefrontal cortex, which is the logical part of the brain. You both will operate solely from an emotional stance, which will make it impossible for your child to truly take in what you are saying (or screaming), and vice versa. This is why yelling or berating your child, will not stir up the confession and repentance you are after.

From a spiritual/emotional perspective, condemnation leads to shame. We do all sorts of things to hide our shame. Adam and Eve used fig leaves. We use defensiveness, deflection, self-justification, humor, compliance, and more. Often one of these is our first defense when called out. Why? Because our first inclination is to hide. But also, anger rises up within us. For some, anger comes out as attacking. For others, anger is suppressed and manifested in other ways, such as withdrawal, an eating disorder, cutting, and suicidal thoughts.

Does this mean we don't approach our kids in their sin or impose boundaries? Absolutely not. But if our aim is their heart, we can't be reckless in the way we handle their sin. Remember we are not the adolescent! But to not act like one requires intentionality that comes only when we are able to tap into the logical part of our brain. And with prayer! We can't do this in and of ourselves, we need the Father's help.

As a parent, my inability to *not* act on my emotions, my inability to redemptively lead my kids, apart from God's grace, drove me to pray more and more. Since then, I've come to realize if I was as strong, capable, equipped, wise and perfected as I wish I were, I would never go to God in prayer. Even still my default is trying to do things on my own. But God "invites us into the living room of his heart, where we can . . . share freely."[2] This is his desire: for us to come and commune with him, to pour out our hearts. This is what it is to live in dependence on him. Again, when we are weak, he is strong (2 Corinthians 12:10).

As we think about entering in with our children in a way that reaches their hearts, I want us to consider how Jesus enters in with sinners. Read here what may be a familiar passage, Jesus's conversation with the Samaritan woman at the well:

> A woman from Samaria came to draw water. Jesus said to her, "Give me a drink." (For his disciples had gone away into the city to buy food.) The Samaritan woman said to him, "How is it that you, a Jew, ask for a drink from me, a woman of Samaria?" (For Jews have no dealings with Samaritans.) Jesus answered her, "If you knew the gift of God, and who it is that is saying to you, 'Give me a drink,' you would have asked him, and he would have given you living water." The woman said to him, "Sir, you have nothing to draw water with, and the well is deep. Where do you get that living water? Are you greater than our father Jacob? He gave us the well and drank from it himself, as did his sons and his livestock." Jesus said to her, "Everyone who drinks of this water will be thirsty again, but whoever drinks of the water

that I will give him will never be thirsty again. The water that I will give him will become in him a spring of water welling up to eternal life." The woman said to him, "Sir, give me this water, so that I will not be thirsty or have to come here to draw water."

Jesus said to her, "Go, call your husband, and come here." The woman answered him, "I have no husband." Jesus said to her, "You are right in saying, 'I have no husband'; for you have had five husbands, and the one you now have is not your husband. What you have said is true." The woman said to him, "Sir, I perceive that you are a prophet. Our fathers worshiped on this mountain, but you say that in Jerusalem is the place where people ought to worship." Jesus said to her, "Woman, believe me, the hour is coming when neither on this mountain nor in Jerusalem will you worship the Father. You worship what you do not know; we worship what we know, for salvation is from the Jews. But the hour is coming, and is now here, when the true worshipers will worship the Father in spirit and truth, for the Father is seeking such people to worship him. God is spirit, and those who worship him must worship in spirit and truth." The woman said to him, "I know that Messiah is coming (he who is called Christ). When he comes, he will tell us all things." Jesus said to her, "I who speak to you am he."

Just then his disciples came back. They marveled that he was talking with a woman, but no one said, "What do you seek?" or, "Why are you talking with her?" So the woman left her water jar and went away into town and said to the people, "Come, see a man who told me all that I ever did. Can this be the Christ?" (John 4:7–29)

Jesus exposed the woman's sin and need, but he did so in a non-threatening, non-condemning way after asking her for a drink. This in itself is remarkable because first, she is female, since at that time men did not commingle with the opposite sex. Second, she was of a despised minority race. Third, she had been married many times and was now living with someone she was not married to. So simply by Jesus not running off as if she were a pariah, he communicated compassion. And before he said anything alluding to her sin and need, he connected with her, which enabled her to have ears to listen. This circles back to the importance of intentional connection. Regularly doing so helps create a connected bond with our children, which positively influences behavior and enhances our ability to correctively discipline. In other words, if we are connected with our child, discipline issues should not be such a struggle.

By the end of the exchange between Jesus and the woman, she left her water jug behind and went to tell everyone about Jesus (a sign that she no longer needed to look elsewhere to be filled). An amazing 180-degree turn after only a brief conversation! Be prepared: our kids likely won't come around so quickly. But as Jesus did with the woman, we will make far greater headway in getting to their true condition and need when we seek to understand what their heart craves (their idol) and how that points to the sin below the surface. Too often, though, parents fly off the handle, imposing punishment without ever dealing with the heart.

Angry teenaged counselees tell me all the time that their phone or something else was taken away or that they are grounded. While I understand the need for consequences and the desire to make them think next time before doing something wrong, these means of discipline do nothing to effectively shepherd their hearts. One reason the teens are angry is not because they don't necessarily know what they did was wrong, but because the means of discipline didn't include identification, entering in or shepherding their hearts. Instead, the means of discipline was distancing which only heightens the relational disconnect. When you learn to discipline redemptively with your young children, it will be a much more familiar part of life by the time your children are teenagers. Of course, any time you discipline a child they are likely to be angry, but you can work through it in a redemptive way instead of a punitive way.

I mentioned the vape story about my son who didn't want to look bad in front of his friends. Had we simply imposed some sort of punishment without probing his heart, we would have fallen into law-based parenting. But through identification, the door was opened to a conversation that led him to repent not just of the behavior, but his idol.

Showing compassion will do more to influence our children's future behavior than punitive discipline. And in showing compassion, our children are more receptive to seeing their need for the intervening work of a compassionate Savior, full of grace and forgiveness. Keep in mind too that our children need to know that no matter what they've done or think, or how awful they treat us, we fully accept and love them.

One way we can affirm our unconditional love for our children is to never leave them feeling separated from us after discipline. My husband talks about how, after being punished as a kid, he would arrange all the cereal boxes around him at the table the next morning so he didn't have to see his parents and they couldn't see him. He hadn't experienced the reality of a clean slate, so he was still hiding in shame. Beyond our own relationships with our children, when we banish them to their rooms without restoration, they assume this too is how God treats them in their sin. But this isn't how God treats us—it is his look of love, his compassion and grace toward sinners, that transforms hearts.

I know that even when we do move toward our children with compassion and grace, they may still respond in anger. I work with many families in which this is the case and know how excruciating it is to feel so disconnected from a child. Though I hope that the proactive, long-range parenting guidance offered in the book helps prevent such power struggles, this won't always be the case. Sometimes God allows hard seasons and rebellion and in no way do I want to minimize how painful and difficult these times are. At the same time, I know God is not removed from us in these trials, and often we can look back on these trials later and see his hand in growing us and our children in grace.

Compassion for Yourself

Can you be okay not being okay? Can you accept that in this world of guaranteed struggle, God is not finished yet with us (or our kids)? That we are in process, and progress is not always linear?

Sitting in the middle of that story is hard. Isn't that why we try to control? Or throw our arms up in despair? Why we doubt God and lose hope?

And yet, Jesus says, "Come to me, all who labor and are heavy laden, and I will give you rest. Take my yoke upon you, and learn from me, for I am gentle and lowly in heart, and you will find rest for your souls. For my yoke is easy, and my burden is light" (Matthew 11:28–30).

In our worries, panic, fear, doubts, uncertainty, sleeplessness, anger, Jesus bids us to unload it all on to him. Not only does he want to carry it; he offers us rest in it. I don't know about you, but when I've gone through challenging times, my mind has rarely been settled. Experiencing rest in the midst of hard is clearly God's grace.

Remarkably, as I am growing in grace, so is my ability to trust God and rest in the unknown. This is completely outside of myself. No way apart from God's work within me could I keep from freaking out when there is trouble with one of my kids. But remember how we talked about the memorial markers? As God has delivered my husband and I through various parenting valleys, another rock has been added to my stack. Even as I write this, we are dealing with something with one of our children, but my mind is not as worked up over the *what ifs* as it has been in the past. And amazingly, I am free from needing to nag and control in this particular instance.

In the messy middle and the long journey of parenting, we must keep our gospel glasses on. And like the farmer from James 5, day after day we remain steadfast in our work with the end goal in mind. As encouragement, I love how Paul Tripp puts it in his book *Parenting*:

> It's important to make the mental/spiritual shift from viewing parenting as a series of unrelated corrective encounters to viewing parenting as a lifelong connected process. Since change is most often a process and seldom an event, you have to remember that you can't look for a dramatic transformation conclusion to your encounters with your children. Seldom is change the result of a dramatic moment. So you have partial conversations and unfinished moments, but in each moment you are imparting wisdom to your child, each moment you are exposing your child's heart, each moment you are building your child's self-awareness, each moment you are giving your child great God-awareness, each moment you are constructing a biblical worldview for your child, and each moment you are giving the Spirit of God an opportunity to do things in and for your child than you cannot do.[3]

All is grace. Still, we keep looking for formulas and quick fixes, hoping for an easier way. But I've come to see the easy path wouldn't do so much for our growth in grace and dependence on Jesus. Nor would it necessarily force redemptive living.

Though we may pick coasting by, God has more in mind for us. For if life is Christ, he will do whatever it takes for us to find our life in Christ.

As we conclude, I hope rather than feeling frustrated that I didn't offer you a fool-proof Christian parenting formula, you feel freed. Knowing that no matter what parenting tendencies you hope to change, the idols you would like to topple, or any other failure, God moves toward you with compassion. I am convinced that how we experience his love and grace and how we place our hope in his truth will directly impact how we live in our families and will, in the long run, directly impact our children.

"Now to him who is able to do far more abundantly than all we ask or think according to the power at work within us, to him be glory in the church and in Christ Jesus throughout all generations, forever and ever. Amen" (Ephesians 3:20–21).

Questions for Reflection and Discussion:

1. How has your understanding of sanctification changed or grown?
2. What has been most challenging for you with addressing sin and discipline issues with your child and how might what you read in this chapter change anything?
3. In thinking over the entire book, what were your biggest takeaways?

Appendix A
The Redemptive Parenting Assessment

FOR EACH QUESTION, indicate your answer by checking the appropriate column: Never, Sometimes, Often, or Always. If you think you may want to reuse the assessment later, or have your spouse also take the assessment, I recommend using a pencil or a separate sheet of paper for your answers.

Questions	Never (1)	Sometimes (2)	Often (3)	Always (4)
I am attentive to my child's physical and emotional needs.				
I regularly address discipline issues as they occur.				
I use threats of discipline but don't carry through.				
I give in to my child to appease them or avert drama.				
I worry that anything other than praise and positive reinforcement will hurt my child's self-esteem.				
I make sure my child understands the reasons behind my expectations, decisions, and rules.				
I allow my child's preferences to determine decisions for our family.				
I stick with the boundaries set for my child.				
I struggle to set boundaries.				
I frequently talk with my child about his/her feelings.				
I give my child the freedom to express his/her own opinion.				
I feel threatened when my child doesn't hold the same opinion or beliefs as me.				
My child is required to do chores.				
When my child doesn't have time to help with chores, I do it for him/her.				
When my child forgets something, I take care of it for him/her.				
I tend to do things for my child that he/she could do for himself/herself.				
If my child is involved in conflict, I get involved.				
First-time obedience is enforced in our house.				
I find myself nagging my child.				
I feel like a bad parent when my child doesn't behave.				
I see my child's behavior, performance, and appearance as a reflection of me.				

Questions	Never (1)	Sometimes (2)	Often (3)	Always (4)
It is hard for me to consistently discipline.				
I prioritize family mealtime.				
I don't want my child to miss out, so I sacrifice my time and schedule to take him/her places.				
I exhibit more of a hands-off approach to parenting.				
My child talks to me about his/her thoughts and emotions.				
My child leans on me to take care of things.				
My child acts in a self-sufficient manner.				
I maintain rigid rules and monitoring in our household.				
I make parenting decisions based on what other parents think is okay.				
I know my child's friends, friends' parents, and teachers.				
I hesitate to enforce rules because I want my child to like me.				
My child's grades are most important.				
My child's athletic or artistic success drives family decisions and conversations.				
I work hard to make sure my child is happy.				
Church attendance and involvement is a priority in our family.				
In our family, we talk about faith and spiritual things.				
I look to my children to meet my needs.				
My life is centered around my children.				
I put my children's needs before my spouse's.				
It is hard for me to ask for forgiveness.				

Questions	Never (1)	Sometimes (2)	Often (3)	Always (4)
I apologize to my child when I have done wrong.				
I spend unstructured "play" time with my child.				
I struggle to connect with my child whose interests are different from mine.				
My agenda or to-do lists for my child dominates our conversations.				

Now take some time to look back over your responses and make note of any observations?

Do you see any areas in which you would like to change or grow? If so, what?

Are there any responses that spark new self-awareness or curious self-reflection? If so, what?

Appendix B
Gospel-Centered Resources for Shepherding Your Children

Ministry Websites

Birds & Bees – Guides parents in how to introduce and continue conversations about sex with their children: https://birds-bees.com

CPYU (Center for Parent/Youth Understanding) – Helps parents understand and respond to the ever-changing culture from a Christian worldview: https://cpyu.org

Defend Young Minds – Teaches parents how to guide their children to reject pornography: https://www.defendyoungminds.com

Harvest USA – Biblical help for individuals and families affected by sexual struggles: https://harvestusa.org

Rooted Ministry – Equips and empowers churches and parents to faithfully disciple teens toward a lifelong faith in Christ: https://www.rootedministry.com

Books and Articles

Church and Theology

First Catechism: Teaching Children Bible Truths (Suwanee, GA: Great Commission Publications, 2003).

Gospel-centered church article: Yancey Arrington, "How Can You Tell If a Church Is Gospel-Centered? Start with the Pulpit," *The Gospel Coalition*, May 29, 2019, https://www.thegospelcoalition.org/article/church-gospel-centered-start-pulpit/.

Marty Machowski, *The Ology: Ancient Truths, Ever New* (Greensboro: New Growth Press, 2021).

Sex, Gender, and Culture

Harvest USA, *Alive: Gospel Sexuality for Students* (Greensboro: New Growth Press, 2018).

Marty Machowski, *God Made Boys and Girls* (Greensboro: New Growth Press, 2019).

Walt Mueller, *God's Plan for Sex and Gender: 10 Teaching Points for Home and Church* (Elizabethtown, KY: Center for Parent/Youth Understanding, 2022), https://cpyu.org/wp-content/uploads/2022/03/Gods-Plan-for-Sex-and-Gender.pdf.

Walt Mueller, *A Student's Guide to Navigating Culture* (Fearn, UK: Christian Focus Publications, 2021).

General Parenting

Sissy Goff, David Thomas, and Melissa Trevathan, *Are My Kids on Track? The 12 Emotional, Social, and Spiritual Milestones Your Child Needs to Reach* (Minneapolis: Bethany House, 2017).

Drew Hill, *Alongside: Loving Teenagers with the Gospel* (Greensboro, New Growth Press, 2018).

Bob Kellemen, *Raising Kids in the Way of Grace: 5 Practical Marks of Grace-Focused Parenting* (Leyland, UK: 10Publishing, 2018).

Julie Lowe, *Child Proof: Parenting by Faith, Not Formula* (Greensboro: New Growth Press, 2018).

Paul David Tripp, *Age of Opportunity: A Biblical Guide to Parenting Teens* (Phillipsburg, NJ: P&R Publishing, 1997).

Lori Wildenberg, *Messy Parenting: Powerful and Practical Ways to Strengthen Family Connections* (Birmingham: New Hope Publishers, 2018).

Books to Shepherd Young Hearts

CCEF's *Good News for Little Hearts Series* (Greensboro: New Growth Press, 2018–2021).

- *Buster's Ears Trip Him Up: When You Fail* by Edward T. Welch
- *Buster Tries to Bail: When You Are Stressed* by David and Nan Powlison
- *Caspian Crashes the Party: When You Are Jealous* by Edward T. Welch
- *Gus Loses His Grip: When You Want Something Too Much* by David Powlison
- *Gwen Tells Tales: When It's Hard to Tell the Truth* by Edward T. Welch
- *Halle Takes a Stand: When You Want to Fit In* by Paul David Tripp
- *Henry's Big Mistake: When You Feel Guilty* by Lauren Whitman
- *Henry Says Good-Bye: When You Are Sad* by Edward T. Welch
- *Jax's Tail Twitches: When You Are Angry* by David Powlison

- *Tori Comes Out of Her Shell: When You Are Lonely* by Jayne Clark
- *Zoe's Hiding Place: When You Are Anxious* by David Powlison
- *Zoe's Time to Shine: When You Want to Hide* by Edward T. Welch

Podcasts

The Redemptive Parenting Podcast with Kristen and Pete Hatton

Raising Boys & Girls with Sissy Goff, David Thomas and Melissa Trevathan

Rooted Parent with Cameron Cole and Anna Harris, produced by Rooted Ministry

Ask Alice with Alice Churnock, produced by Rooted Ministry

Youth Culture Matters, produced by Center for Parent/Youth Understanding

Acknowledgments

THIS BOOK WAS a long time coming—an idea tabled for several years so I could pursue grad school. Eager to write again, I proposed the idea soon after finishing my master's without fully knowing what the road to licensure for a counselor truly entailed. Looking back, it was not the most ideal time to start a new manuscript, but I was excited to dive in, and my dear husband, instead of squelching my enthusiasm, once again entered into a crazy season with me. (Made even crazier when we learned around the time of the editing process that we would be uprooting and moving states!) Pete, thank you for standing by my constant stream of new ideas and cheering me on at every twist and turn. And for being the best dad I could ever have hoped for our children. How grateful I am to have a husband and co-parent who leads and lives redemptively with us.

Rebecca, David, and Jonathan, as children of a pastor-dad and writer-mom, your stories often become the experiences we draw upon. Thank you for allowing me to sprinkle bits and pieces of those stories—your stories—into this book. And for loving and forgiving me and Dad when we failed you and didn't parent you as you needed. You three reflect Jesus to us, and nothing makes me prouder than being your mom.

To my mom and dad, Sheryl and Doug Bech, and my in-laws, Jean and Chris Hatton, thank you for raising me and Pete in the faith and prioritizing family. Your love for Jesus, for each other, and your children gave me and Pete the best foundation and legacy to pass on to our children, and their children to come. Also, a special thanks to my new friend, Rachel Craddock, for volunteering to read through the first draft of this book, offering editing expertise and perspective as a *before-the-teen-years* mom. Your insight and encouragement were a well-timed gift to me.

Thank you, too, to my Oklahoma counseling supervisor, Kyle McGraw, for allowing me the space and time to write and encouraging me in my pursuit to proactively assist parents and families before crises erupts.

Last but certainly not least, I am grateful for my ongoing relationship with New Growth Press. Barbara Juliani, thank you for continuing to entertain my ideas and offer me opportunities. To Ruth, Cheryl, Audra, and the rest of the team: you make the process smooth, and the final product and delivery even better than I could imagine. I am so grateful.

Endnotes

Introduction

1. Kristen Hatton, "8 Things Parents Can Do Now to Shape the Teen Years Ahead," *Kristen Hatton* (blog), June 4, 2017, https://www.kristenhatton.com/8-things-parents-can-now-shape-teens-years-ahead/.

2. Kristen Hatton, "Before the Teen Years: Getting to the Heart of Sin with Our Kids," *Kristen Hatton* (blog), June 11, 2017, https://www.kristenhatton.com/teen-years-getting-heart-sin-kids/.

Chapter 1

1. Paul David Tripp, *Age of Opportunity: A Biblical Guide to Parenting Teens* (Phillipsburg, NJ: P&R Publishing, 1997), 14, 19.

2. Tripp, *Age of Opportunity*, 22.

3. Tripp, *Age of Opportunity*, 23.

4. Merriam-Webster, s.v. "*proactive (adj.)*," accessed February 5, 2022, https://www.merriam-webster.com/dictionary/proactive.

Chapter 2

1. Julie Lythcott-Haims, *How to Raise an Adult: Break Free of the Overparenting Trap and Prepare Your Kids for Success* (New York: St. Martin's Griffin, 2016), 43, 74.

2. Kristen Hatton, *Exodus for Students: The Gospel-Centered Life* (Greensboro: New Growth Press, 2017), 93.

3. Hatton, *Exodus for Students*, 103.

4. Barbara Duguid, *Extravagant Grace: God's Glory Displayed in Our Weakness* (Phillipsburg: P&R Publishing, 2014), 128.

5. Merriam-Webster, s.v. "*behold (n.)*," accessed February 5, 2022, https://www.merriam-webster.com/dictionary/behold.

6. John Newton, "Amazing Grace" (1779), *Timeless Truths*, accessed February 7, 2022, https://library.timelesstruths.org/music/Amazing_Grace/.

Chapter 3

1. Nathan A. Winner and Bonnie C. Nicholson, "Overparenting and Narcissism in Young Adults: The Mediating Role of Psychological Control," *Journal of Child and Family Studies* 27, no. 11 (2018): 3650–57.

2. Chris Segrin et al., "Parent and Child Traits Associated with Overparenting," *Journal of Social and Clinical Psychology* 32, no. 6 (2013): 569–95.

3. Ming Cui et al., "Parental Indulgence, Self-regulation, and Young Adults' Behavioral and Emotional Problems," *Journal of Family Studies* 25, no. 3 (2019): 233–49.

4. Ming Cui et al., "Parental Indulgence: Profiles and Relations to College Students' Emotional and Behavioral Problems," *Journal of Child and Family Studies* 27, no. 8 (2018): 2456–66.

5. Sarah N. Wolford et al., "Examining Parental Internal Processes Associated with Indulgent Parenting: A Thematic Analysis," *Journal of Child and Family Studies* 29, no. 3 (2020): 660–75.

6. Cui et al., "Parental Indulgence, Self-regulation," 233–49.

7. Evin W. Richardson, Leslie G. Simons, and Ted G. Futris, "Linking Family-of-Origin Experiences and Perpetration of Sexual Coercion: College Males' Sense of Entitlement," *Journal of Child and Family Studies* 26, no. 3 (2017): 781–91.

8. Richardson, "Linking Family-of-Origin Experiences," 782.

9. Ming Cui et al., "Indulgent Parenting, Helicopter Parenting, and Well-being of Parents and Emerging Adults," *Journal of Child and Family Studies* 28, no. 3 (2019): 860–71.

10. California Department of Education, "Parenting Style Questionnaire (PSQ), *Parent Engagement Module Series* (Sacramento: California Department of Education, 2020), https://www3.cde.ca.gov/pem/module2/story_content/external_files/ParentingStyle Questionnairev8.pdf; Focus on the Family, *7 Traits of Effective Parenting Assessment* (Colorado Springs: Focus on the Family, 2018), https://assessments.focusonthefamily.com/s3/7-Parenting-Traits-Assessment?utm_source=www.focusonthefamily.com&utm_medium=referral&utm_campaign=article_cta_7traits&refcd=798506.

Tim Elmore, *12 Huge Mistakes Parents Can Avoid: Leading Your Kids to Succeed in Life* (Eugene, OR: Harvest House Publishers, 2014), 11–13.

Chapter 4

1. Tim Keller, *Counterfeit Gods: The Empty Promises of Money, Sex, and Power, and the Only Hope That Matters* (New York: Penguin Books, 2009), xvii.

2. John Calvin, *Institutes of the Christian Religion*, ed. John T. McNeill, trans. Ford Lewis Battles (Philadelphia: Westminster, 1960), Print [Institutes 1.11.8], 108.

3. Paul David Tripp, *Instruments in the Redeemer's Hands: People in Need of Change Helping People in Need of Change* (Phillipsburg, NJ: P & R Publishing Company, 2002), 85–86.

4. Kristen Hatton, *The Gospel-Centered Life in Exodus for Students* (Greensboro, NC: New Growth Press, 2018), 98.

Chapter 5

1. Kristen Hatton, *Get Your Story Straight: A Teen's Guide to Learning & Living the Gospel* (Greensboro: New Growth Press, 2015), 10, 34–35.

2. Christian Smith and Ann Adamczyk, *Handing Down the Faith: How Parents Pass Their Religion on to the Next Generation* (Oxford: Oxford University Press, 2021).

3. David Briggs, "The No. 1 Reason Teens Keep the Faith as Young Adults," *Huffington Post*, October 29, 2014, https://www.huffingtonpost.com/david-briggs/the-no-1-reason-teens-kee_b_6067838.html/.

4. Kristen Hatton, "What Are We Feeding Our Families?," *Risen Motherhood* (blog), January 14, 2019, https://www.risenmotherhood.com/blog/what-are-we-feeding-our-families/.

Chapter 7

1. Megan Michelson, "Talking to Your Kids about Sex," *The Redemptive Parenting Podcast*, podcast audio, May 20, 2020, https://redemptiveparenting.org/podcasts/guest-episode-talking-to-your-kids-about-sex-with-megan-michelson/.

Chapter 8

1. David Briggs, "The No. 1 Reason Teens Keep the Faith as Young Adults," *Huffington Post*, October 29, 2014, https://www.huffingtonpost.com/david-briggs/the-no-1-reason-teens-kee_b_6067838.html/.

2. Kristen Hatton, "Behind a Counselor's Door: Why Kids Don't Talk to Their Parents," *Rooted Ministry* (blog), June 16, 2022, https://rootedministry.com/blog/behind-a-counselors-door-why-kids-dont-talk-to-their-parents/.

3. Paul David Tripp, *Instruments in the Redeemer's Hands: People in Need of Change Helping People in Need of Change* (Phillipsburg, NJ: P & R Publishing, 2002), 34.

4. Tim Keller, *The Prodigal God: Recovering the Heart of the Christian Faith* (London: Penguin Books, 2011), 29–47.

5. Aaron Earls, "Most Teenagers Drop Out of Church When They Become Young Adults," *Lifeway Research*, January 15, 2019, https://research.lifeway.com/2019/01/15/most-teenagers-drop-out-of-church-as-young-adults/.

Chapter 9

1. Kristen Hatton, *Face Time: Your Identity in a Selfie World* (Greensboro: New Growth Press, 2017), 1.

2. Kristen Hatton, "Behind a Counselor's Door: Why Kids Don't Talk to Their Parents," *Rooted Ministry* (blog), June 16, 2022, https://rootedministry.com/blog/behind-a-counselors-door-why-kids-dont-talk-to-their-parents/.

3. The ideas in this section were inspired by a TBRI training I attended: Cindy R. Lee, "Collaborative Impact Project TBRI Training," HALO Project International, Oklahoma City, 2021–2022.

4. Karyn Purvis and David Cross, TBRI, 1999–2021.

Chapter 10

1. Julie Lowe, *Child Proof: Parenting by Faith, Not Formula* (Greensboro: New Growth Press, 2018), 81–82.

Chapter 11

1. Cindy R. Lee, "Making Sense of Your Past Worth: Participant's Guide," (Oklahoma City: HALO Project International, 2018), 14.

2. Richard J. Foster, *Prayer: Finding the Heart's True Home* (New York: HarperCollins Publishers, 1992), 1.

3. Paul David Tripp, "Parenting Is a Process," *Crossway* (blog), July 30, 2021, https://www.crossway.org/articles/parenting-is-a-process/.